. . . . AND HE WILL BE
YET WISER *Proverbs 9:9*

TEACH YOURSELF
EMBROIDERY

is one of

THE E.U.P. BOOKS

published by the

ENGLISH UNIVERSITIES PRESS

THE **EUP** BOOKS

The first seven titles

THE E.U.P. STUDENT'S GUIDE

THE E.U.P. TEACH YOURSELF FRENCH

THE E.U.P. TEACH YOURSELF MATHEMATICS

THE E.U.P. TEACH YOURSELF EMBROIDERY

THE E.U.P. TEACH YOURSELF GOOD ENGLISH

THE E.U.P. SPEAKER AND DEBATER

THE E.U.P. TEACH YOURSELF LATIN

In active preparation

THE E.U.P. TEACH YOURSELF GERMAN

THE E.U.P. STANDARD ELOCUTIONIST

THE E.U.P. HOUSEHOLD DOCTOR

THE E.U.P. TEACH YOURSELF TO COOK

Further volumes will be added

TEACH YOURSELF
EMBROIDERY

A BOOK OF SELF-INSTRUCTION IN THE ART OF
EMBROIDERY PREPARED UNDER THE DIRECTION
OF MARY THOMAS, AUTHOR OF MARY THOMAS'S
EMBROIDERY BOOK AND MARY THOMAS'S
DICTIONARY OF EMBROIDERY STITCHES

THE ENGLISH UNIVERSITIES PRESS
WARWICK SQUARE, LONDON, E.C.4

First printed in this form 1938

*Printed in Great Britain for the English Universities Press, Limited,
by Richard Clay and Sons, Limited, Bungay, Suffolk.*

PREFACE

EMBROIDERY is the art of enriching a fabric by stitchery. It is not only a pleasant pastime, but a practical means of making garments appear more luxurious and the home more beautiful.

Most materials can be embroidered in some form or other, and when cost has to be considered, this is a rather satisfying thought. Moreover, experience reveals that much of the so-called costliness associated with embroidery is more often due to work begun and never finished, or scampered through so that it is worthless, than to any initial outlay.

Some embroideries are expensive. To wit—Church embroideries, ceremonial embroideries. But what of the peasant embroideries which by common consent rank among the most beautiful in the world? These are done by the poorest of people and on some of the coarsest materials. In their own country they are rarely without their work in their hands. Each stitch is added with care, and the work is not expected to be finished in five minutes! This would be waste of good material! A shocking offence.

These peasant embroideries are used mainly to decorate wearing apparel and household articles, and the average woman of any country still desires to make the same use of her work. This little book is planned with this objective. First to show how simple stitches, which we have known from childhood, can be used with beautiful effect in embroidery, and secondly—since fashion so largely dictates our mode of dress—how embroidery can be used to impart an exclusive look to dresses, lingerie and household articles, in such a way that their value is accordingly enhanced by the addition of the stitchery.

There are many different ways of doing this, and the student is advised to read this book straight through from beginning to end, in order to get a comprehensive understanding of the subject, and then settle down to serious study.

MARY THOMAS.

CONTENTS

	PAGE
NEEDLES, THREADS AND FABRICS	9
WHAT IS EMBROIDERY?	15
POTTED WISDOM	19
EMBROIDERY STITCHES	21
TYPES OF EMBROIDERY	55
DOUBLE RUNNING EMBROIDERY	57
CROSS STITCH EMBROIDERY	63
ASSISI EMBROIDERY	69
ROUMANIAN EMBROIDERY	75
DARNING EMBROIDERY	77
APPLIED WORK	83
PATCHWORK	93
QUILTING	100
SMOCKING	110
BRODERIE ANGLAISE	118
CUT WORK	128
DRAWN THREAD WORK	136
LETTERING	144
DECORATIVE STITCHING AND FAGGOTING	149
TRANSFERS, FRAMES AND WASHING	159
INDEX	163

With love to Joyce
    from Grandpa.

WBaird

Christmas 1939.

LESSON I

NEEDLES, THREADS AND FABRICS

IN teaching yourself embroidery, be fair to yourself and use proper implements, the principal of these being embroidery needles. They cost but a fraction more than ordinary needles, but since they are specially designed with large eyes (in order to protect the working thread) and sharp points (the good ones), an amateur trying to embroider with an ordinary needle places herself under a severe handicap.

Why?

All embroidery threads, silk, wool or mercerised cotton, are more loosely " twisted " than sewing silks, cottons or darning wools, as their objective is to " cover a flat surface," and not to join seams or mend holes. This loose twist enables the thread to " spread " or " cover " more easily, but at the same time the strands are more exposed, and so apt to fray or break more easily. By using an embroidery needle, which is easily threaded, the strands are more loosely confined, and the long eye admits the easy passage of the thread without strain. Also the work proceeds more easily.

9

During work it is also advisable to move the position of the needle, so that the thread does not get worn in any one particular place. An expert embroidress will straighten out her thread, adjust the position of the needle from time to time, and at the same time roll the needle lightly between her fingers (rolling in one direction only). This re-twists the working thread (wool, silk or cotton), which, because of its loosely twisted nature, easily becomes straight. Only a few twists are necessary. Always look after your threads, because these are the medium of expression in embroidery. Never use a frayed thread. It spoils the effect of the embroidery, so discard it immediately and take a new length.

Kinds of Needles

There are three kinds of embroidery needles— Crewel needles, Chenille needles and Wool needles.

Crewel needles are those in general use. They are long and sharp and easily threaded. Several sizes are included in one packet, and the size which best admits the embroidery thread should be chosen.

The Chenille needle is shorter and the eye larger, and is generally preferred when the embroidery is worked on a frame.

The Wool needle has a blunt point, and is used for embroidering on net or canvas, also on coarse linen when the threads are being counted.   Also for whipping and lacing embroidery stitches.

All three kinds of needles should be bought and used as required.

Threads

Be practical in your choice of embroidery threads. Use linen cotton or mercerised threads on linen or cotton materials.   Silk on silk, wool on wool. They wash better, because they are spun to the same tension and have the same pull.

On articles which are not so frequently in the wash, this rule can be slackened.   Touches of silk embroidery can be used on a woollen frock, and wool on linen cushions and runners—the latter with this proviso, that there must be a relationship between the two, using a fine crewel wool, or heavy embroidery wool, according to the texture of the fabric.   Mercerised cottons have a certain sheen, and look effective on delustered materials, such as dull satin, crêpe-de-chine, georgette, etc.

Remember that all embroidery threads have a loose twist, as explained, and that this unfits them for any sewing action.   Therefore in doing such works as Quilting, Smocking or Faggoting, which are a compromise between sewing and embroidery, use a more firmly twisted thread, one of the " Pearled " varieties in silk, or a buttonhole twist.

Lastly, but most important, buy only FAST colours, as faded embroidery looks shabby.

Fabric Choice and Treatment

Choice of fabric is important, as a good fabric inspires good work. But don't outclass yourself, or the effect of living up to the fabric will spoil the spontaneous joy of the work. Begin on a practice fabric. Buy a yard of hand-woven linen 18 inches wide, and use this as a sampler on which to experiment all the different stitches and effects required. Hand-woven peasant linen costs very little.

On a fabric of this type the threads of the warp and weft can be easily counted, and regularity in length of stitch learnt from the start.

Fashion Fabrics

Fashion largely dictates the choice of dress and lingerie materials, the desire for chic governing any practical selection. On these the embroidery should last as long as the material. This means simple embroideries on inexpensive materials, and elaborate on elaborate materials. Vary the working thread, silk or cotton, according to the fabric.

Cotton embroidery threads will last as long as any cotton fabric, but the constant washing demands simple short stitches. Consider the peasant embroideries which are usually in Cross Stitch. In choosing silk or crêpe-de-chine lingerie materials, buy the best you can afford, but it is only wasted effort to attempt lavish embroideries on a fabric of poor quality. Moreover, the fine work will actually tear the fabric in wear, and so fail in its mission of being decorative. This is a misuse of embroidery. On no occasion ever use the embroidery thread too heavy, as this always weakens the fabric. Sheer linen will take fine embroidery, just like good crêpe-de-chine. Also the best rayon materials.

Household Fabrics

Fabrics for household articles are naturally chosen to last, so always buy fast colours. This is the most important consideration when buying for household use. A harsh material is tiring to work upon, so is better avoided. With this advice, many materials will be found which are suitable for embroidery.

All fabrics can be embroidered in some form or other, and once you are acquainted with your stitches and a few types of embroidery, it is easy to see the possibilities and scope for work which different materials offer.

If an unusual material is chosen, then the stitches must be adapted to suit the fabric. If, on the other hand, you wish to do a particular type of work, then the material on which this is best expressed should be chosen.

This is taking a practical view of things, and embroidery *is* practical—at least, household embroidery. If you want to do fine work, buy fine materials; if coarse work, then buy coarse material.

First Piece of Work

Don't start off with a bedspread once the sampler is completed! The work on this may not be more difficult, but the task becomes wearisome and the work, if ever finished, develops into a grim effort.

Embroidery is meant to be a pleasure. Let the first choice be a mat, or luncheon set, cushion or runner—something that can be visualised as finished before the first stitch is made. This is so much more encouraging and interesting. After this the bedspread won't seem at all grim.

For floral designs a transfer is the simplest solution. In order to get a desired effect it is sometimes necessary to buy a large transfer and cut out the required portion. Any transfer can be cut and redistributed as desired, leaving out those portions which are not required. Two transfers can be united or certain portions of different transfers, as required. Never be a slave to any one transfer design, unless of course it pleases.

Designs treated in this way become much more personal, and the mind more alert, as it is always on the look-out for ideas. Always be on your toes for these.

If the material is transparent, it can be placed over any design and the outline pencilled in.

Some good effects can be obtained on self-printed fabrics, or silks, like brocade, by embroidering certain portions of the pattern. Cretonnes and printed silks can be treated in the same way. This idea used on dress materials is most effective. The material for, say, the sleeves of a dress could be made to appear quite different by outlining the design in Running Stitch, using a different tone or contrasting colour. It should be varied, according to the design. For instance, the flower centres could be given another colour by covering them with Satin Stitch or French Knots, treating the larger flowers differently from the small, or doing only one and not the other.

This is putting embroidery to practical use, making the fabric richer because of the added stitches, and so adding to its intrinsic value in a gratifying manner. All forms of embroidery should have this objective.

POTTED WISDOM

A needle with a worn eye will fray the embroidery thread and cause it to ravel.

The rough edge of a thimble will do the same, so both should be discarded.

Cheap needles quite frequently have rough eyes—so don't buy them.

A crooked needle will make a crooked stitch. Throw it away.

All embroidery threads, silk, wool or cotton, should be cut and not broken.

When an embroidery thread tends to fluff or lose its freshness, take a new length.

Use sharp embroidery scissors. Blunt ones will jag your threads and your materials.

Keep your embroidery work handy in a wrapper and spread this over your lap when working.

Don't put two different kinds of work in the same wrapper. They get jumbled together and cause unnecessary annoyance.

viduality and a pleasing choice of stitch, which, properly applied to the right purpose, is one of the governing factors of good embroidery.

No illustration, however perfect, can impart this knowledge, as a drawing is only an eye knowledge, and not that felt by hand and sense.

Order of Stitches

The following stitches have been arranged in progressive order so that it can be seen how a simple stitch can become a compound stitch, by using the simpler form as a foundation for additional ornament. This not only changes its appearance, but also its name, which should be memorised. It will be noticed, too, that embroidery stitches are not always worked in the same direction, as while some stitches are worked from right to left, others are worked from left to right.

LESSON 1

LINE STITCHES

These are the simplest stitches, and used to form straight lines, also outlines, and, when worked close together, can be used as fillings (see Fig. 8).

Running Stitch (Fig. 1)

The simplest of all embroidery stitches is Running Stitch, which every needlewoman can work.

Each stitch must be of equal length, and travel over three or four threads of the material, picking up only one or two threads in between each. The

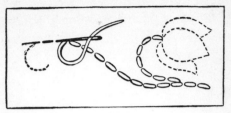

Fig. 1.

effect is a slightly broken line of stitches, and as such it is much used as a line stitch, also for outlining and as a foundation for composite stitches.

Running Stitch—Whipped (Fig. 2)

Running Stitch can be given a greater importance by whipping it, as shown in Fig. 2. Use a

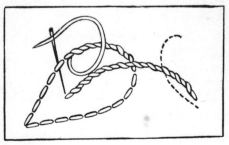

Fig. 2.

blunt wool needle and overcast each stitch, inserting the needle downwards through the top of the stitch without penetrating the material at any spot.

Holbein Stitch or Double Running Stitch (Fig. 3)

This stitch is a cousin in the Running Stitch family, but is technically known as Holbein Stitch, and should be remembered as such. The working method is shown in Fig. 3, and in two different

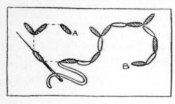

Fig. 3.

coloured threads, so that its construction can be followed. It differs a little from ordinary Running Stitch, as the needle travels over and under the same number of threads, and to form it into a solid line of stitching as shown, two journeys are necessary. The first journey begins at *A*, with the dark thread, and travels round to *B*. Here the work is turned and the second journey made, this time the thread travelling over the spaces left on the first journey, and under the previous stitches. Holbein Stitch can be used as a line stitch and for outlining. When used as a motif, it is often made with little stitches offshooting as shown. This is further explained in Double Running Embroidery (see p. 57).

Back Stitch (Fig. 4)

There are two methods of working this stitch, but both are worked from right to left as shown.

Method 1. The needle is brought out a short distance from the beginning of the line to be covered (see arrow in the diagram), and is inserted again at the beginning of the line, thus taking a step " back," to emerge an equal distance beyond

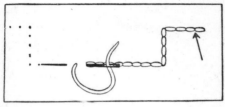

Fig. 4.

the point where it first started, as shown in the diagram. Repeat.

Method 2. The needle is brought out at the commencement of the line and inserted at the arrow, four threads in advance. It then travels under four threads and emerges. For the next stitch insert the needle again at the arrow and come out again at the same spot as the thread. From here travel over four and under four. This builds up a line of back stitching on the front, as shown in Fig. 4, but on the under side a line of Running Stitch, and as such is Back Stitch used in

25

Quilting. Back Stitch can be used as a line stitch, also as a foundation for other stitches.

Threaded Back Stitch (Fig. 5)

This shows Back Stitch treated as a foundation stitch and threaded, which imparts a braid-like effect, especially if a thicker thread is used for the

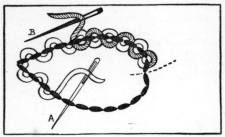

Fig. 5.

purpose. The stitch can be threaded with a matching or contrasting colour as shown, and can be threaded once, as at *A*, or twice, as at *B*. Use a fine wool needle for the threading.

Pekinese Stitch (Fig. 6)

This is another and very famous method of threading a Back Stitch, as Pekinese Stitch is renowned in Chinese embroideries. The loops in the design are a little exaggerated so that the working method can be seen; in reality the thread is drawn quite firmly to form a fancy line stitch, which is used as such or as a filling. If a metal

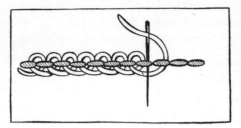

Fig. 6.

thread is used for the lacing, then the broad, braid-like effect, as shown, is effective.

Stem Stitch (Fig. 7)

Stem Stitch is a sort of back stitch worked from left to right. The needle emerges at the end of the line to be covered. It then enters the material

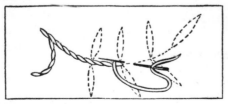

Fig. 7.

a little farther along to the right, and emerges again a short distance towards the left, thus making a long step forward and a short step back. The

27

Sham Hem Stitch (Fig. 10)

The foundation of this stitch is really a herring-bone movement, but worked from right to left, as shown in Fig. 10. Bring the needle out at *A*, insert it at *B*; bring it out at *C*, insert it at *D*; bring it out again at *E*, and so on. The second thread is then laced over these foundation stitches

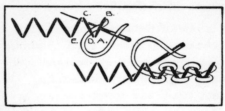

Fig. 10.

in the manner shown, without piercing the material except at the beginning and end of the line. This stitch can be worked over a run-and-fell seam in lingerie or anything similar in fine material, to make an effective covering for the seam line, and at the same time imitate the effect of a hemstitched seam. Also used as a border stitch.

LESSON 3

LOOPED STITCHES

It should be noticed that in forming these stitches the needle is always brought through *over* the working thread, and that they are invariably worked from left to right. There is: (1) simple loop, such as Blanket Stitch; (2) fancy loop, such as Feather Stitch; (3) complete loop, such as Chain Stitch.

Cretan Stitch (Fig. 11)

For this stitch the needle is inserted vertically, instead of horizontally, as in Herringbone Stitch, and is drawn through over the working thread.

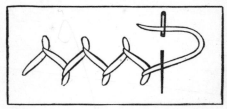

Fig. 11.

The upper stitch is formed as shown, the needle being inserted downwards. The stitch in the lower line will be made by inserting the needle vertically, but upwards.

Blanket Stitch (Fig. 12)

This is worked as shown from left to right. The needle is brought through on the bottom line (*A*), and inserted above, on the top line, a little to the right, and out immediately below, drawing the needle through over the working thread. Continue as shown in the diagram. Blanket Stitch is worked the same as Buttonhole Stitch, only spaced apart. It can be used as a decoration in circular form, as at *A*, or to cover the edge of a turned

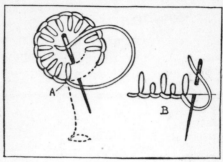

Fig. 12.

under hem, as on blankets. This is a more familiar use, and at *B* is shown a simple variation, the stitch being alternately long and short. It can also be arranged in groups of two or three stitches with larger spaces between each group, or two long and two short stitches, and so on.

Buttonhole Stitch (Fig. 13)

Working from left to right, the thread emerges on the lower line, and the needle is inserted and brought out again as shown, and pulled through over the working thread. This forms a long, straight stitch with a closely looped edge on the lower line, which is exceedingly useful in Cut Work, as the tight, closely placed loops prevent

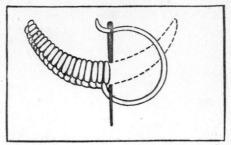

Fig. 13.

fraying when the material is cut away. Also used for Scalloping, for working bars, in all forms of Cut Work, and is, in its own right, a decorative stitch, and used for floral forms, line stitches, borders, etc.

Buttonhole Stitch Wheel (Fig. 14)

This is an effective way of arranging Buttonhole Stitch in circular formation so

Fig. 14.

C

that it " pulls " a central hole in the fabric. The effect is derived by taking each stitch into this same central hole.

Closed Buttonhole Stitch (Fig. 15)

This is another variation of Buttonhole Stitch, worked from left to right and in the same way,

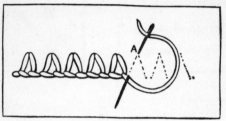

Fig. 15.

except that the needle enters the material at the spot *A*, for each pair of stitches.

FANCY LOOP STITCHES

This group of Loop Stitches are fancy free in design, and in shape, and form a sort of half or open loop.

Single Feather Stitch (Fig. 16)

This is the simplest version of a very famous family of Loop Stitches. The thread is brought through at the top of the line to be worked and held down with the left thumb. The needle is then inserted in a slanting direction as shown in the diagram and pulled through over the working thread. This process is repeated throughout. Single Feather Stitch is often used in smocking.

Fig. 16.

Feather Stitch (Fig. 17)

This is a little more elaborate, as the stitches branch left and right. The needle emerges at the top of the line to be covered and takes a stitch a little lower down to the right at an angle, and is

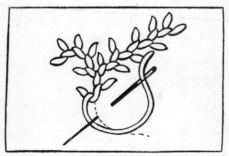

Fig. 17.

then pulled through over the working thread. A similar stitch is then made on the left side of the

35

line, and the work is continued in this way, alternately to right and to left. This is a favourite stitch for decorating babies' and children's garments, and can be used almost anywhere for a line or border. The stitch, as seen, very closely resembles the effect of Coral, and under this name it is sometimes known.

Closed Feather Stitch (Fig. 18)

Although very different in effect, the working method for this stitch is the same as for ordinary

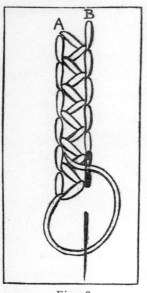

Fig. 18.

Feather Stitch, only the needle enters the material at a different angle and always close up to the last stitch. The thread emerges at *A* on the left side of the line to be covered, and is then thrown and held, while the needle enters the material on the right at *B*, a little higher up, and emerges again below, as in the diagram. It is then pulled through over the working thread, which is then thrown over to the right, and the needle inserted just below the commencement of the first stitch, when the second stitch is made in the same way. The process is continued in this way, each new stitch being made so close to the last that an almost unbroken line results on the outer edges. It will be noted that the stitches are not opposite each other, as the top of one coincides with the centre of that opposite.

Double Feather Stitch (Fig. 19)

This attractive variation of ordinary Feather Stitch is a general favourite. Instead of making single stitches alternately right and left as in Fig. 17, two or three stitches are made consecutively on one side and a similar number on the opposite side, to build up a pretty zigzag line. For special effects it can be worked irregularly, arranging two stitches to one side, four to the next, three to the next, and so on. The stitch is much used on babies' layettes and children's clothes, and is also

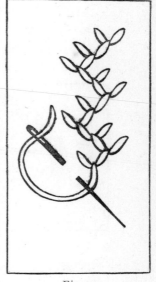

Fig. 19.

37

used to obtain light feathery effects in any type of embroidery.

COMPLETED LOOP, OR CHAIN STITCHES

This group of stitches is as renowned and versatile as the Feather Stitch group, and concludes the Loop family, which began with the simple loop as an edging in Blanket Stitch, and developed into a half loop as in Feather Stitch, and now becomes a completed loop or Chain. Remembered in this way, this working method will never be forgotten.

Chain Stitch (Fig. 20)

The thread is brought out at the top of the line to be covered and held down on the material to the

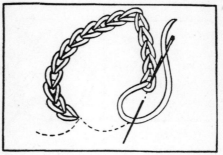

Fig. 20.

left and with the left thumb. The needle is then inserted into the same spot where the thread first emerged and is brought out a short distance below (according to the length of stitch required). It is then drawn through over the working thread as shown in the diagram, and so forms a complete loop. The stitch is repeated thus, always ensuring that the needle enters the same hole as that through which the thread emerges, and that the stitches are of equal length. Chain Stitch builds up a line of back stitching on the reverse side of the material, and is used for Quilting, as a line border stitch, or as a filling (worked in close rows) and as a padding when raised effects are required in Cut Work, Scalloping, Lettering, etc.

Zigzag Chain Stitch (Fig. 21)

This is a pleasing variation of Chain Stitch, worked in the same way, only each chain loop is made at an angle to the last to produce a zigzag

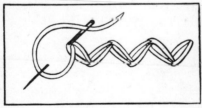

Fig. 21.

line. In order to keep the loop flat and in position, the needle must pierce the end of each loop as it enters the material (see diagram). Used for borders and lines.

Daisy Stitch or Detached Chain Stitch (Fig. 22)

This most popular stitch is really composed of single or detached loops of Chain Stitch. The thread must emerge at the required spot for the stitch and be held down a little to the left with the left thumb. The needle is then inserted again into the same spot, and emerges below at the required length of the stitch. It is then drawn

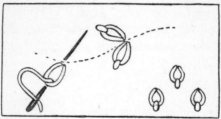

Fig. 22.

through over the working thread, and the loop thus formed is secured by a stitch taken over the end of the loop as in the diagram. The needle will then emerge in position for the next loop. Daisy Stitches may be used to simulate leaves and flower petals, also as a filling, spacing the stitches evenly apart as shown on the right.

Magic or Chequered Chain Stitch (Fig. 23)

This is worked with two threads of contrasting colour threaded together into one needle. Commence working exactly as for ordinary Chain

Stitch, but when the needle is ready to be pulled through over the two threads, remove the dark thread from beneath the needle point (see diagram) and pull through over the light thread only. The second stitch is as the first, only the colours are

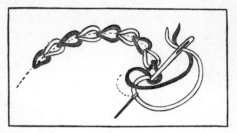

Fig. 23.

reversed and the white thread is lifted from beneath the needle point, and the stitch made is black. If some of the contrasting-coloured thread is still showing on the surface, a slight pull will cause it to disappear.

Open Chain Stitch (Fig. 24)

The appearance of Chain Stitch is considerably altered by changing the angle of the needle as shown. The thread emerges at A and is held down with the left thumb. Insert the needle exactly opposite and let it emerge again just below A, as shown, and pull through over the working thread. The loop thus formed must be left a little

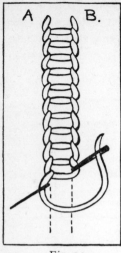

Fig. 24.

slack, as in making the second stitch the needle is inserted just inside it on the right-hand side, as in the diagram. This stitch is used for borders and broad lines. Also as a casing for ribbon on lingerie.

Fly Stitch (Fig. 25)

Fly Stitch is formed by detaching the loops of an Open Chain Stitch. Imagine the stitch to be worked on a **V** shape with the thread emerging at the top of the left arm. The needle is then inserted again just opposite at the top of the right arm, and emerges at the base of the **V**, and is pulled

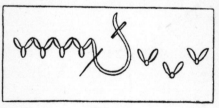

Fig. 25.

through over the working thread as in the diagram. The loop thus formed is then tied with a small stitch taken into the material below. This final " tying "

42

stitch may vary in length as shown. A small tie stitch is shown on the detached stitches to the right, and longer ones in the group to the left, where it looks like the letter " Y " and is sometimes known as Y stitch.

Fly Stitch Filling (Fig. 26)

This shows how to use Fly Stitch to form a trellis-like filling. A row of Fly Stitches is worked as shown in Fig. 25, but in the second row the fly stitches are inverted and placed so that the

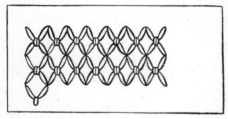

Fig. 26.

tying stitches of the second row come alongside those of the first row and link the two in the form of an oblong cross. The rows are repeated thus, touching each other, to form the filling. Experiment will produce many other effects.

FLAT STITCHES

These are special stitches used to cover large or small shapes. They lie flat upon the surface, and depend on strict regularity for effect. Flat Stitches have less character than other stitches, but are exceedingly popular, because they can be shaded to give realistic colour effects, as in painting. The most famous are the Satin Stitches.

Overcast Stitch (Fig. 27)

Overcast Stitch is really the narrowest form of Satin Stitch. The line to be covered must first be run stitched as in the diagram. The needle then travels over and beneath this, picking up a thread or two of material and making the stitches very close together to present a firm raised line. This

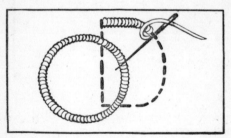

Fig. 27.

stitch is much used in all types of embroidery, but especially for working stalks, stems and outlining floral shapes, etc. It is shown here on a mono-gram, for which purpose it is most suitable, especially when worked with linen thread on linen, etc.

44

Satin Stitch (Fig. 28)

Although this appears one of the simplest of embroidery stitches, it is actually one of the most difficult to work correctly and neatly, and should be thoroughly mastered. Satin Stitch is formed by carrying the thread across the space to be filled and returning beneath the material a thread beyond the starting point, ready for the next stitch. The

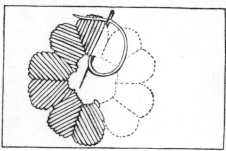

Fig. 28.

stitches must lie even and closely together and preserve a neat, firm edge to the shape which is being filled. The Satin Stitches may be worked in any direction and be of any length, but a very long stitch becomes unwieldy and untidy. In filling any large shape it should be split up into convenient sections, see rose-petal in the diagram. The smaller spaces are then filled, changing the direction of the stitch. Such change imparts an effect of light and shade, even though the colour of the thread remains the same. This is the charm of the stitch, and explains its name—satin.

Surface Satin Stitch (Fig. 29)

This is an economical method of working large shapes in Satin Stitch, as all the thread is kept on the surface. Instead of inserting the needle and carrying it beneath to the opposite margin, a tiny stitch of one or two threads is picked up as shown, and the thread carried over the surface and a

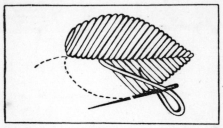

Fig. 29.

similar stitch on the opposite side, and so on. The method is not very satisfactory, as it is difficult to make the stitches lie close to each other. This may be avoided to some extent by picking up a slightly larger stitch, leaving a small space between each stitch, which is then filled in by making a second journey over the whole form, and filling in the space left on the first journey.

46

Padded Satin Stitch (Figs. 30 and 31)

Small shapes to be covered in Satin Stitch can be given a better and more definite outline when they are first emphasised with Running Stitches made first within the line of the design (see Fig. 30). This also gives a slight sense of relief. A more

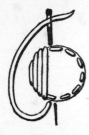

Fig. 30.   *Fig. 31.*

pronounced relief is given as in Fig. 31. The shape is first padded with Satin Stitches made within the outline, as shown. These are then closely covered with Satin Stitch. Used on all forms of embroidery, especially Broderie Anglaise.

Whipped Satin Stitch (Fig. 32)

A raised or corded effect can be obtained by whipping over a filling or line of ordinary Satin Stitch. The Satin Stitches should be slanted and the Whipping Stitches placed almost at right angles and slightly apart. Used for leaf fillings, heavy stems, etc.

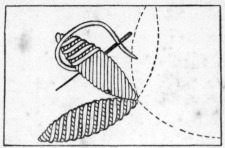

Fig. 32.

Long and Short Stitch (Fig. 33)

Long and Short Stitch is worked exactly like ordinary Satin Stitch, and derives its name from

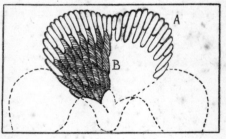

Fig. 33.

the irregular method of commencing the work, as shown at *A*. After completing the outline in this manner, Satin Stitches of equal length are fitted

48

into the spaces left on the first journey and continued until the shape is filled, as at *B*. The length of the Satin Stitch remains the same, except where variation is required for filling uneven shapes. The stitch is particularly useful for shading, as a lighter or darker tone may be fitted into the irregular spaces, or, to use the technical word, encroached, to effect a gradual shading from one colour to another, without any strongly defined line. Although Long and Short Stitch is often regarded as one of the simpler embroidery stitches, considerable care is necessary in grading the stitches, in order to form a neat and satisfactory finish.

KNOTTED STITCHES

The most popular stitches in this big family are French Knot and Bullion Knot, both being formed by a process of knotting.

French Knot (Fig. 34)

Bring the thread through at the spot where a knot is required, and hold down firmly with the left thumb and first finger, the material being held meanwhile with the second and third fingers of the left hand. The needle is then twisted two or three times over the thread, as shown by the upper needle in the diagram, and then, with the twists pulled nearly tight upon the needle and the thread still held firmly in the left hand, the point of the needle is turned completely round as shown by the direction of the arrow in the diagram, and inserted at the dot in the diagram close to where the thread first emerged. The needle is then pulled through the twists to the back of the material, or, if the knots are being worked in a line, it can emerge again at the required spot and

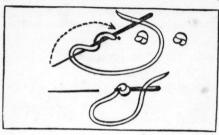

Fig. 34.

the pulling through be done in one movement, as shown by the lower needle. Many people find a difficulty in making these stitches correctly, the secret of successful work being the twist of the needle and the taut thread. French Knots are used as fillings for flower centres, etc., for tiny powdered patterns and anywhere that the effect of a single dot is required, as for eyes, etc.

Bullion Knot (Fig. 35)

This is a far more elaborate knot, and somewhat tricky to master. First bring the thread through at the spot on the diagram marked by the arrow. Insert the needle back the required length of the stitch and to the right as at *A*, and let it emerge again exactly at the arrow. Do not pull the needle right through, but leave it lying thus in the material, and twist the thread round and round it close up to the emerging point. Six or seven twists are an average number, but these should be varied according to the length required. Place the left thumb

Fig. 35.

upon the twists, and pull the needle and thread carefully through the material and also through the twists. Now pull the needle and thread away in the opposite direction. This forces the little coil to lie flat and in its proper position. Pull the working thread to tighten, and then pass the needle through to the back at *A*. This spot should coincide with the end of the bullion knot, providing the correct number of twists have been made to fill up the space. Bullion Knots require a little practice before they can be made perfectly, and should not be attempted with a very fine thread until they have been first mastered in a coarse one. Use a rather thick needle with a narrow eye, a crewel needle, so that it will pass easily through the twists. Bullion Knots are shown in the diagram at B as forming the petals of a flower. They are particularly suited to this and also to form small flowers, etc.

The " Porto Rico Rose "

This consists entirely of Bullion Knots arranged in a coil to form a small rosebud. To get the effect the knot is not laid flat, but allowed to hoop a little. Used as a decoration on lingerie, etc.

COUCHING STITCHES

These are special stitches used in a special form of embroidery, two of which, as shown here, are very popular and can be used with good effect as required.

Couching (Fig. 36)

What is meant by Couching is shown in this diagram, where four black threads are being sewn or " couched " down with a white thread. This is the simplest Couching Stitch. The four threads are all brought through to the right end of the line to be covered, and then allowed to lie upon the material. Holding these with the left thumb, bring out the white thread at the spot marked by the arrow, and take a tiny upright stitch over the bunch of threads, bringing the needle out farther along ready for the next stitch. The threads which

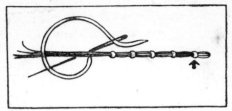

Fig. 36.

are being couched must be held firmly, and not allowed to loop or pucker, while the Couching-down Stitches should be made firm and not too far apart. One thick thread or a cord can be couched in the same way. Used as a line, outline or border, and found in appliqué embroidery, etc.

Roumanian Couching (Fig. 37)

This is quite a different method of work, as the thread being couched and that doing the work are one and the same. The method is exceedingly useful for filling long spaces, leaves, backgrounds, etc.

A long stitch is first thrown across the space to be filled, as follows. The needle emerges at *A* on the left of the shape and is taken across and inserted at *B*, emerging at *C* as shown. This long thread is then couched down with loose slanting stitches,

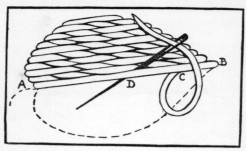

Fig. 37.

as in the diagram at *D*. These stitches must not be pulled tight, and should be long enough and sufficiently slanting to be almost indistinguishable from the original long stitch they are tying down.

Random Note

Just as Patchwork is a means of using up all odd scraps of material, so is Picture embroidery, garden scenes, etc., a means of using to advantage all left-over embroidery threads.

TYPES OF EMBROIDERY

THE following chapters explain different types of embroidery, such as will be found useful for decorating dress or household articles.

The lessons are simply explained and easily followed. The first three lessons are important, as they show constructional development, revealing how a simple embroidery can become more elaborate by amalgamation, just as simple embroidery stitches become compound stitches in the same way. The embroideries start off in the same way as the stitches, with one of the Running Stitches—namely, Double Running Embroidery.

The idea of counting the threads of the fabric in order to ensure strict regularity of stitch often appears a formidable task to the beginner, and were fabrics of very fine weave used, there might be reason for this thought. But such works are mainly of peasant origin, and in consequence worked on hand-made linen, on which the threads can be easily counted, and this custom should be followed by the worker, until at least the principles of the different works have been mastered.

The worker should regard her fabric in the same light as an artist regards his canvas—as something to be decorated—and study it accordingly, giving considerable thought to it before the first stitch is made, and then the layout and effect when finished will be very much more interesting.

Reversible Embroidery

RUNNING STITCH as noted is the simplest of all embroidery stitches, but when it is employed in Double Running Embroidery it must be spaced equally apart, counting the threads and picking up a regular unit of, say, three threads of the material and passing over three threads as in Holbein Stitch. The work is done in two journeys, and this is the first journey. On the second or return journey the stitch is made in the same way, but passing over the threads that were missed on the first journey, and so beneath the stitch previously made, thus resulting in a complete unbroken line of stitches, the same on the back as on the front. Two journeys have been made, so the line is Double Run, and the work known as Double Running.

Design

A straight line constructed in this way is often used for dress decoration, but Fig. 38 shows how this simple little stitch can be built to form a lovely lace-like design. As in all embroideries constructed on the counting principle, we must look for the basic line of construction, when attempting to reproduce any design such as shown in Fig. 38. This is shown to the right with the first journey only completed. Watch how this line winds its way through the whole design, carrying little

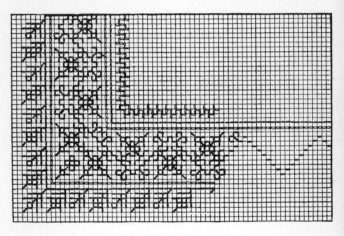

Fig. 38.

offshoots and motifs at regular intervals. Notice also how each stitch is either horizontal or vertical, and never diagonal. This is the characteristic charm of the design, which would lose much of its beauty were this angular formation lost.

Other patterns of this description can be planned out on graph paper, as that shown in Fig. 38 is

58

planned, treating each square as a unit. For experiment make the fundamental line of battlement formation, or simplified Greek Key pattern with appropriate offshoots to fill the spaces. Remember it is this fundamental line which carries the whole design.

Working Threads and Materials

As regularity of stitch is imperative, it is important that the warp and weft of the material be of even degree and loosely woven, in order to count the threads without undue eye-strain. White, cream or natural-coloured linens are best, and the working thread used for the embroidery must be about equal in thickness to the warp and weft of the material, and is better made with a loose cable twist. A fine, blunt-pointed wool-needle can be used, in order not to split the ground threads.

The embroidery is generally worked in one colour, black on white being very popular, and dark brown on a fawn linen. The colour should be strong, such as red, green, blue, yellow. Two or more colours can be used if desired.

LESSON

The fundamental line must be well placed upon the linen. If a border on a mat is being considered, then begin in the middle of one side, and work this line right and left. The corners will then present no difficulty.

The method of working the embroidery is shown in Fig. 39. A unit of three threads is sug-

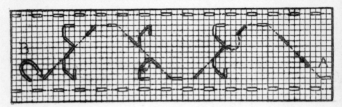

Fig. 39.

gested, as this odd number appears more pleasing. Commence at *A* on the right and form the fundamental line, making each stitch and space of equal length. The dotted lines show where the needle

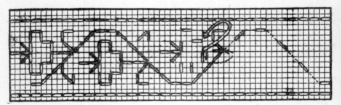

Fig. 40.

is taken beneath the material. After a little experience some of the little offshoots can be added on this first journey. Upon reaching the spot for an " offshoot," work right to the end of the

60

branch and return again to the main outline. The dotted arrows indicate the procedure, while at *B*, the white arrow indicates the commencement of the second journey, which is shown in detail in Fig. 40. This is the most exciting, as the spaces left on the first journey are filled in to make a continuous line, each stitch fitting into its own particular place. Fig. 40 shows that further " off- shoots " are added on this second journey, but whether these are worked in on the first or second journey, or some on both, must depend on the construction of the design.

Notice in these figures the fundamental line is diagonal, and in consequence the offshoots will take a diagonal formation, as the lines are com- plementary. The angular formation, as in Fig. 38, is the best and simplest, and this should be the first aim of the student.

The great thing to remember is that the back of the work should look just like the front, and when working any secondary motifs or offshoots, the thread must keep to the outline of the design on the back, and not be carried across a space or allowed to " cut " a corner; otherwise an un- wanted stitch alien to the design appears and spoils the effect. The work is meant to be reversible.

The best method to commence and finish off is to run in the end of a new thread on the right side, weaving it under and over single threads of the material along the outline of the design for a short distance, and cover this with the Double Running Stitches.

An important point to remember when working the second journey is to insert the needle in the same hole, but just above the thread of the stitch made on the first journey, and bring it out below, or vice versa, as this makes all the difference between a good and bad line. A little experiment will soon show the effect of this.

Random Notes

Hedebo is a Danish peasant embroidery, done in Cut and Drawn work, usually on a coarse hand-woven linen.

o   o   o

Drawn Fabric work is not the same as Drawn Thread work. In the first the special stitches are tightened to pull the fabric in small perforations; in the second, the warp and weft threads are withdrawn and those remaining gathered together, as in Hemstitching.

o   o   o

Black embroidery is a Spanish work done in black thread on white linen. Katharine of Aragon, the Spanish wife of Henry VIII, introduced it into England.

SOME of the most beautiful peasant embroideries in the world are done in Cross Stitch, many in one colour only, others almost startling, both in colour and design. A typical example of Cross Stitch from Roumania is shown in Fig. 41.

The beauty of this embroidery depends on the strict regularity of each stitch which is achieved by counting the threads of the material. No transfer will ever give the same results as counting, as it is well-nigh impossible to offset it with such accuracy, and the stitches are crooked. Work of this kind will not enrich the fabric. On such materials as crêpe-de-chine or satin, where the weave does not show, a transfer can be used, but it lessens the interest of the work, and Cross Stitch, being of peasant origin, was never intended for such luxury materials.

Working Materials

All fabrics must have an even warp and weft, which can be easily seen and counted, such as linen, voile, hessian, hopsac, and some of the modern furnishing materials where the weave is almost $\frac{1}{4}$ inch wide. A printed check material can be

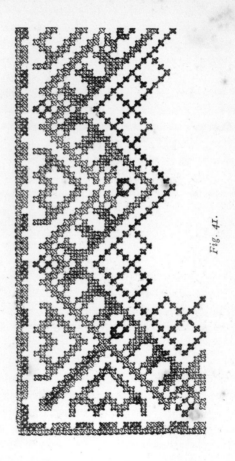

Fig. 41.

adorned with Cross Stitch, using the square as a unit instead of counting the threads.

Any thread, mercerised, silk, woollen or linen, can be used, providing a balance is maintained with the background material. A coarse material necessitates a coarse thread, and vice versa. Stranded cottons are useful, as they can be divided. If embroidery wools are used, the stitches should not be pulled quite so tight as when using cotton threads.

LESSON

Each cross is a separate unit and is square in shape. This is why the material must have an even warp and weft. A unit can comprise any number of threads, counting three threads to the right and three up (a three and three unit), or it can be four and four, or five and five, and so on, making the unit proportionate to the material. On some of the classical pieces the unit is only one!

The stitch is made by bringing the thread through as in Fig. 42. Count three threads across and then three threads down, and insert the needle upwards as shown. This forms half the stitch, and the cross is completed by counting three threads to the left, the needle emerging in position for the next stitch, which in this case is adjoining. If an interval is wanted between each cross, then miss two or three threads and bring the needle

E   65

out as required. The same applies when working
a diagonal line, as featured in Fig. 41.

In forming different shapes it is often necessary
to work a few stitches thus from left to right in
one line, and on the line above or below work
from right to left. The method of forming a
cross as worked from right to left is shown below
in Fig. 42. Study these two carefully, as it shows

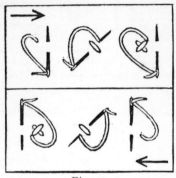

Fig. 42.

that no matter which way the stitch is worked, the
upper thread must always be in the same direction,
from left to right, as in handwriting. If a stitch
crosses in the wrong direction, the light on the
thread is deflected differently, causing it to stand
out like a mistake.

Very large patterns and long border lines of
Cross Stitches can be worked as in Fig. 43, the first
half of the cross being worked in one journey,

and the second half added on the return journey.
The methods of working from right to left or

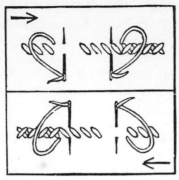

Fig. 43.

from left to right are both shown, so that the
upper thread will always slant to the right, as
directed.

Design

In attempting to copy a design in Cross Stitch
such as shown in Fig. 41, first study the design
carefully, and then choose the salient line as the
first to be worked. In this case it is a broad zigzag line, the inner single black line being the basic
line of construction. This consists of fourteen
crosses worked in a diagonal line, sloping upwards
to the right, and then fourteen sloping downwards.
This one line must be first worked across the width
of the material. If a corner is needed, then turn

as shown, working sixteen stitches and curving in again with the zigzag line of fourteen. Once this is completed, it is quite simple to build up the remainder of the pattern on this fundamental line, using the colours as suggested—black, blue and red.

By following these rules and first finding the basic line of construction, any Cross-Stitch pattern, no matter how complicated it appears, can be reproduced with ease, and of course original designs invented, as it is this one fundamental line which carries the structure of the whole pattern. The colour scheme can be simple, such as black, red and blue. Work the black crosses in Fig. 41 in black, the broad band in red, and the small triangular motifs blue.

On picture charts, especially prepared for Cross Stitch, the colour scheme is often given by the aid of different symbols, which are noted below with explanation.

Random Notes

In Rhodes work the background only is embroidered in Drawn Fabric stitches, and the design left clear.

ゝ   ゝ   ゝ

Stump work is embroidery in relief. Small figures of birds and animals are first stuffed and applied to the background. Human figures are dressed in great elaboration with jewels, beads, and sometimes real hair.

CROSS STITCH AND DOUBLE RUNNING COMBINED

THE subjects of the two previous lessons, Cross Stitch embroidery and Double Running embroidery, can be united as a single work, since they are both constructed on the unit principle. There are two classical methods of doing this, and with such effect that the works are known by different names : (1) Assisi Embroidery, and (2) Roumanian Embroidery. The treatment of stitches in either is the same, but the treatment of design is very different.

ASSISI EMBROIDERY

Heraldry in Embroidery

The chief features of Assisi Embroidery is (1) the design, which is invariably of heraldic character, and (2) treatment, the background only being embroidered, leaving the design clear on the linen, like an intaglio. The work is dignified and looks effective on banners, cushions, bags, tea-cloths, etc.

The embroidery technique is, as explained, a combination of Cross Stitch and Double Running, and all the rules pertaining to these works are applicable to Assisi Embroidery, together with the following special points.

Design

This being the important feature of the work, it must be considered separately. The designs can

Fig. 44.

be first prepared on graph paper, in outline only, each line following the outline of the squares on the paper, either vertically or horizontally, but never diagonally (see Fig. 45, which shows how the diagonal line forming the bird's back is achieved

Fig. 45.

by a series of little steps). If any diagonal line were used, it would divide a square, and so be impossible to fill with a complete Cross Stitch.

Almost any heraldic form can be reduced to

71

this kindergarten method of presentation with but little effort, as experiment will show. The normal outline of any figure could be easily adapted by using a transparent graph paper, or by first tracing upon ordinary graph paper, and adapted afterwards. Constructional lines only are allowed within any figure forming the design, and Fig. 44 shows how few these are.

On the lion, the eye, mane, top of the legs are indicated, and on the bird, the eye and wing. It will be appreciated that the solidity of the background in Cross Stitch forms an abrupt finish at the edges. This is usually softened by a light filigree design, worked in Holbein Stitch. Two suggestions being given, top and bottom, in Fig. 44.

The artist should compare the designs created for Assisi Embroidery with those of Roumanian Embroidery (Fig. 46), as the rules covering stitches and technique are exactly the same, but the method of treating the design—embroidering the background in the first and the motif in the second—gives a strikingly different effect. The designs are not interchangeable, as the intaglio effect needs to be bolder.

The weave of the fabric, coarse or fine, and the unit of the stitch decide the size of the design. Each square represents a unit, and each unit must be the same size and contain the same number of threads to the stitch. A design can be reduced in size by reducing the size of the unit from, say, three threads to two threads. This will reduce it by one-third. To increase the size, increase the size of the unit.

Working Materials

A fabric of even warp and weft must be used on which the threads can be easily counted, white or natural linen being the usual choice. The embroidery thread should be in two different colours only, using a black, brown, green or red for outlining the design, in Holbein Stitch, and a light, contrasting shade for the background of Cross Stitches. In this work, colour is subsidiary to design, so it should be mellow rather than obtrusive, as this gives the work a soft antique appearance.

LESSON

The design is first outlined with Holbein Stitch, as in Double Running Embroidery, so read the instructions for this work. Begin by finding the centre of the design and the centre of the material. By this way the design is placed centrally on the fabric. The unit must also be considered in proportion to the material, the uneven unit of three threads being usually chosen for the size of the stitch. This same unit will govern the size of the Cross

Stitches used to fill in the background. Be careful not to make the unit so big that the design will not go on to the material. Count out 1 inch of units, and then calculate the size on the material.

In making the second journey of Double Running, be careful to insert the needle, as explained, above the stitch and bring it out below. It is better to work the entire design in outline, as in Fig. 45, before beginning the background. The bird in Fig. 45 is a close-up of the central motif at the base of Fig. 44, and shows the treatment of the eye and wing, each little square being first outlined and then filled with a cross. The markings on the lion's neck, mane, eyes, etc., are all treated in the same way.

The method of filling in the background with Cross Stitch is also shown in Fig. 45, one half of the cross being worked first, the second half of the stitch being added on a second journey. See Cross Stitch Embroidery. Be careful to fill in the whole background completely, leaving no spaces or half crosses. Isolated Cross Stitches should be worked as separate units.

When the background is completed, arrange the surrounding border of Holbein Stitches, making this in proportion to the space to be filled. A line of Cross Stitch is sometimes also used as an immediate surround (see Fig. 44). If little sprig motifs are being used, also begin the first in the middle of the line, so that it is centrally placed, and from here work left and right. If the corner motif does not fit nicely, a change can always be made here, and with good effect.

ROUMANIAN EMBROIDERY

In this case the motif is worked as a solid mass of Cross Stitch, and the design given a light, delicate effect of tiny scrolls in Holbein Stitch.

The effect is very charming, but very different from Assisi Embroidery, and can be done in one colour, or in many different colours. The work is found in most Slav countries, though notably in Roumania. In a very gay colour scheme the Holbein Stitch would be in black.

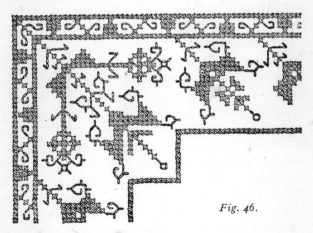

Fig. 46.

LESSON

In a monocolour scheme the little offshoots are added in at the same time as the crosses. The unit for both stitches must be the same, usually three threads. The design can be planned out on graph paper as explained for Cross Stitch and Double Running, but a simple design such as in Fig. 46 could be planned on the material. The basic line of this design is, it will be noted, a series of diagonal lines arranged at intervals along a border. From these branch out little " V " shaped motifs in Cross Stitch, ornamented and bisected by small sprig motifs, in Holbein Stitch.

Reflections

These three lessons have been treated progressively in order to show the principle of development in embroidery, and at the same time to show how nationality affects the appearance of the work, even when the same stitches are used. The Slav method of combining Cross Stitch and Holbein Stitch is accomplished in peasant style, but in Italy, where the principles of design are influenced by the classic, these simple stitches as used in Assisi Embroidery take on quite another effect. As the study of embroidery progresses, the student will become aware of these things herself, and so derives a real pleasure in comparing and discovering the different national treatments of different embroideries, for her own satisfaction.

DARNING STITCH, one of the most overworked and abused stitches in the world, can, when treated properly, become a stitch of dignity and refinement, as seen in Fig. 47, where it is shown used as a background to a motif on muslin; and when a light touch of self-embroidery is wanted on a dress or an undergarment of transparent material, this simple stitch can be used with good results.

LESSON

Use fine thread and a fine, long crewel needle. Darning Stitch as used in embroidery is shown in Fig. 48, where a long stitch is taken over the surface of the fabric, and only a thread or two of the material are picked up between each stitch. By this method the maximum of thread is kept on the surface. Each stitch must be kept strictly regular, and this is best achieved by counting the threads of the material and following along the weave of the fabric.

In Fig. 47 Darning is used as a background, and the bottom needle shows how the stitch must span the design at the back in order to leave it clear and defined. Strict regularity is essential, or the work becomes restless and loses much of the soft, elusive appearance which is its chief charm. The long strands spanning the back of the flower are held in place by the interior marking of the flower-centre. If desired, the outline of the design can be given prominence by an outline of Stem Stitch (page 27), as shown by the upper needle in Fig. 47.

Fig. 47.

The same motif as that in Fig. 47 is shown in Fig. 49, but this time it is the motif which is darned, and not the background. The effect is very different. Three different treatments of the stitch are shown. The leaves to the left are darned vertically and horizontally, following the weave of the material,

and disregarding any interior markings; while to
the right the same vertical and horizontal method

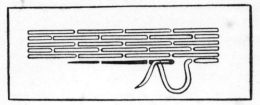

Fig. 48.

is combined to emphasise the centre vein and give
contrast of light and shade.   The flower shows the
stitch worked at right angles to the outline of each

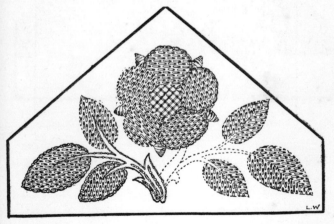

Fig. 49.

79

petal, and this again induces contrast of light and shade. This play of light on the different angles of the stitches is akin to a change of colour in other forms of embroidery.

Huckaback Darning

This is another form of darning, and quite effective as a decoration to hand towels. It is simple to work, as the darning stitches are only threaded under the loops of the huckaback towelling. These loops must be parallel to the selvedge edge.

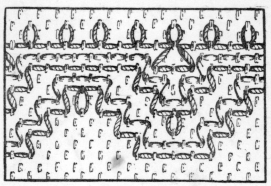

Fig. 50.

Notice this, as in some fabrics the loops are at right angles.

Borders such as shown in Fig. 50 can be of any depth, and have better effect when in contrasting colour to the background. Several shades of one colour are most effective used in one border, using a different shade for each row.

LESSON

Use a long wool needle, and double or single thread, according to the size of the loops. The working method is clearly seen in the illustration,

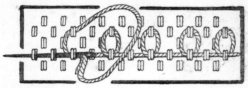

Fig. 51.

the needle being merely slipped under the loops without taking it to the back of the material. To join or finish, run the thread in alongside a previous

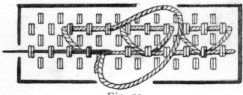

Fig. 52.

line of darning. A study of Fig. 50 will show that the lines of darning are broken by looped and triangular shapes to give interest to the pattern. The method of working the loops or picots is

F   81

shown at Fig. 51, and the triangles at Fig. 52. In both cases the auxiliary decoration is worked in continuously with the darning, carrying the thread first round the shape, and then again under the same little loop, to continue with the main outline of the design.

Random Notes

In Shadow work, certain stitches are worked on the back of a transparent material, and so show on the front as " Shadows."

ᴏ ᴏ ᴏ

Trapunto is worked like Italian Quilting, only in floral designs, the petals being afterwards lightly padded by drawing cotton wool through the under-fabric with a crochet hook.

ᴏ ᴏ ᴏ

Mountmellick embroidery is a white work of Irish origin. The designs are floral and the stitches are chosen to interpret the characteristic appearance of the flower.

ᴏ ᴏ ᴏ

Venetian embroidery is an elaborate form of cut work.

ᴏ ᴏ ᴏ

Lacis is another name for darning on filet net.

Appliqué, Felt Appliqué, Lingerie Appliqué, Net Appliqué

IN Applied Work or Appliqué the design is cut out of one material and applied to the background material by means of decorative stitches, as in Fig.

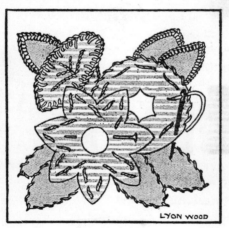

Fig. 53.

53. The design can be in different-coloured materials, as in Fig. 53, but the shapes must be bold and simple in outline. The chief interest of the work

83

lies in the colour of the applied design, which, being of fabric, is flat, as in poster designs. Any colour as supplied by the embroidery stitches is a secondary consideration. The work can be small or large, the scope ranging from miniature motifs on lingerie to colossal figures on theatre curtains !

Working Materials

The applied material need not be of the same kind as the background, but must be of a type that does not fray easily, otherwise the work is not a success. For practical household articles such as table-cloths, mats, pillow-slips, etc., it is advisable to apply linen to linen, as it is stronger, and these articles are frequently in the wash.

For other articles, such as cushions, screens, curtains, etc., the applied fabrics could be velvet, silk, furnishing fabrics, satin, etc. For lingerie, crêpe-de-chine, satin, georgette. When the design is in strong colours, the background material should be of a neutral shade, leaving all contrast to the applied motifs.

The working thread can be silk, mercerised cotton or wool, varying according to the material. Each different motif should be applied with a matching thread or one to tone. On some colourschemes it is effective to use one working thread which matches the background, to attach all the motifs.

LESSON 1

Before beginning any Appliqué work, study the warp and weft of the material and make certain that the applied pieces correspond. Any motif applied on the bias to the ground fabric will " pull " in a contrary direction, causing it to wrinkle, a catastrophe which can only be corrected by cutting a new motif. When a transfer is used, be careful about this when offsetting the different motifs.

In large pieces of work first transfer the design to the background. Then cut out from the transfer the motifs which are to be applied. Lay these on their respective fabrics and cut carefully to shape round the edge of the paper. In special Appliqué transfers, the motifs are given in duplicate, so this is not necessary.

A simple design, such as in Fig. 53, could be evolved easily without the help of a transfer by first cutting each shape out in paper, and using these as a pattern to cut out in material. Many effective shapes and designs can be evolved by drawing round coins, glasses, leaves, petals, etc.

When the shapes are all cut out, arrange each in its correct position, and fasten down with a pin and then tack in position (see Fig. 53). Next lightly overcast the edge of each motif as shown, to prevent it fraying. Notice the method of doing this in

Fig. 53. The needle is inserted downwards. This prevents the motif riding.

This completes the preparation, and the decorative stitches are now added, a process which permits of great individual treatment. A large variety of stitches are available for the purpose, but Button-

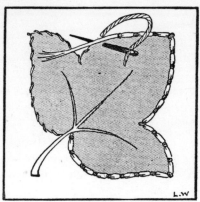

Fig. 54.

hole and Blanket Stitch are the most popular (see Fig. 53). Padded Satin Stitch is also effective. Couching (Fig. 54) is always popular, and on bold designs, used on screen and curtain, braid ribbon and chenille can be couched with great success.

LESSON 2

The technique of Felt Appliqué (Fig. 55) is a little different, as here we are dealing with a non-fraying material, so there is no need to protect the edge of each motif with closely worked stitches.

The design and motif must be simple in outline, and Fig. 55 shows how few stitches are necessary to hold it in position. The long flower-stalk is attached with widely spaced Blanket Stitches.

Fig. 55.

The semi-circular band with serrated edge has single stitches, placed over the narrowest parts. The flowers and leaves are attached in similar simple manner, the method being clearly illustrated. Each stitch should be chosen to do its job properly, without overdoing it, as this gives more character to the work.

This sort of applied work is purely decorative, and while suitable for screens, blotters, pictures, etc., it is not practical on cushions, as the motifs would curl in use, unless more firmly attached.

Lingerie

Appliqué, as used on lingerie, blouses, etc. (Fig. 56), needs to be dainty if it is to portray that " exclusive " look which is the aim and object of most

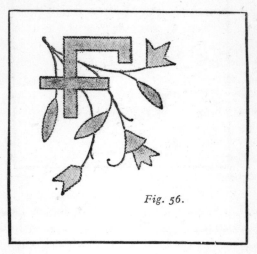

Fig. 56.

needle-women. This is best achieved by applying the motif in Lace Stitch, or, to use the popular French name, Point Turc, which makes the work sound so important. This stitch—point means

88

stitch—imparts an open, lace-like effect to the work.

Only fine materials, such as crêpe-de-chine, georgette, ninon, lawn, sheer linen, should be used. In choosing crêpe-de-chine, select the soft kind, as some, even expensive ones, are so closely woven that the work becomes tiring.

LESSON 3

The design is offset and the motif cut out and tacked in position as explained in Fig. 53, but no preliminary overcasting is necessary or desirable, as it would interfere with the lace stitch. This builds up a double row of stitches and can be worked directly over, and as close as possible to the raw edge of the material. Any frayed ends are neatly trimmed afterwards.

Lace Stitch or Point Turc

A thick " Punch " needle and fine thread must be used. The thick needle is necessary to punch a large hole each time it enters the material, and the fine thread is not meant to show. The perforations form the decoration. Two stitches are made over each other, taking the needle twice into the same holes, while the fine thread is pulled tight after each stitch so that the material is drawn aside to leave a small open space. This in repetition builds up a double line of small holes similar in effect to hemstitching.

The working method is shown in Fig. 57, and the spaces between each stitch should be as regular as possible. Bring the needle through at *A*, insert it at *B*, and bring it out again at *A*. Draw the thread tight and repeat. Next insert the needle at *C*, and bring it out at *A*—this is the position of the needle in the diagram. Make two stitches here,

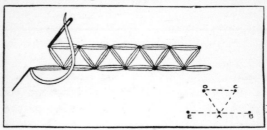

Fig. 57.

drawing both tight, and then insert the needle at *C* and bring it out at *D*. Afterwards insert it at *D* and bring it out at *A*. Next insert it at *A* and bring it out at *E*. Continue in this way as shown until the motif is completely attached.

Experiment should be made on an odd scrap of material in order to get an even " pull " to the stitch and the spacing equal. This stitch can also be used with good effect on the single material for working motifs, stalks, etc. It is often used on linen, in which case the threads can be counted.

This stitch really belongs to the Drawn Fabric family, and is used in that form of work.

LESSON 4

A touch of net is always a nice finish to any dainty garment. A net hem, such as shown in Fig. 58, is applied in the following way. The order of work and preparation is a little different, as the material is cut away round the motif, after it has been attached to the net ground with embroidery stitches,

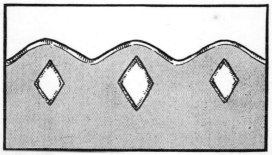

Fig. 58.

and not before, as in other forms of Appliqué. The material is therefore carried over on the net for this purpose.

The net is folded double to form the hem. The design is offset on the fabric, the design in Fig. 53 being a simple scallop with small diamond motifs below it. The material is then laid over the double net and all three are tacked securely together. After this a running stitch must be worked through all three materials, just inside the outline of the design. The running stitches are then covered with fine Satin or Overcast Stitch. Button Stitch is also sometimes used, but which ever stitch is chosen, the needle must penetrate all three layers of material. This is important if the work is to last.

When all the embroidery is completed, and not before, the tacking threads can be removed and the surplus material below the scallops and round each motif carefully cut away. If possible, use ball-pointed lace scissors, as these do not catch in the net. If other embroidery is needed inside the motif, then this also must be worked before the material is cut away; as this avoids any possibility of pulling the motif out of shape in the working.

Random Notes

Decoupé is an inverse form of Appliqué work, as the design is cut out of the linen and a coloured patch put beneath, and attached with buttonhole stitch worked over the cut edges.

o   o   o

Hardanger embroidery is a Norwegian work, usually in white on white canvas-like linen. The designs are mainly geometric, and the more elaborate forms have open spaces

PATCHWORK

PATCHWORK is one of those dear old-fashioned forms of work which have sprung suddenly into favour again. What is more, it is the oldest and best form of Patchwork which has been revived—namely, Geometric Patchwork.

How much this work was beloved by the thrifty folk of those long-ago days—and how ambitious the undertaking! No article was too big. Curtains, bedspreads, loose covers for chairs, etc., etc., all inspiring specimens, many of which yet linger for our admiration and education.

Working Materials

Any odd scrap of material, plain or patterned, can be used for this work, though it is not advisable to mix silks and cottons on any one piece of work, as the heavier cotton materials will shorten the life of the silken fabrics, and after washing, the silk patches will incline to wear badly. Let the work be either composed of all cotton fabrics or all silk fabrics. Moreover, try to keep them all the same weight by not mixing thin and thick fabrics (cotton or silk) together on any one work. Uniformity of kind should be the aim. The sewing-cotton used for joining the patches should be strong, but at the same time bear some relationship to the weight of the fabric. Use a fine cotton with fine materials and vice versa. Keep a special reel of cotton for the work, and use the same throughout. This also makes for uniformity of strength.

LESSON

COLOUR AND DESIGN

Colour is an important consideration in Patchwork, and it is well when sorting out the pieces to arrange them in colour groups. Keep some definite colour in mind as a background, and arrange the strong colours to form high lights.

A study of *B*, Fig. 59, will show that three colours have been grouped together. For convenience we may call these Red, White and Blue; the centre being Red, the strongest colour; with two whites and four blues. The latter will form a background colour. There are seven patches altogether. By making another group similar to this, and joining the white to the white, and continuing in this way a straight border line, comprised of two white patches alternating with one red, would be evolved. A border line of this description on, say, a bedspread has a good effect, and gives meaning to the design.

When the border line is complete, make groups

94

of sevens in other shades for the middle. In uniting them, these can be made to form a diamond in the centre. For the outside border, group seven patches of darker colours together. It is far more convenient to work in this way preparing seven patches at a time, and uniting the groups together afterwards, as with a little care and manipulation some surprisingly good results can be derived.

Geometric Shapes

In Geometric Patchwork each patch must be cut to some regular geometric shape, the most popular being : (1) the Scale (see *A*, Fig. 59), and (2) the Hexagon (*B*, Fig. 59).

In order to cut these shapes, it is necessary to have a model shape. This can be cut out of cardboard (or bought in tin), and is called a " Template." Fig. 59 shows how to construct both the Scale and the Hexagon templates. Both are based on the circle. Take a compass (or pin and string) and with a radius of, say, $1\frac{1}{2}$ inches describe a circle. (Try it out on paper first, to test out the size required.)

For the Scale Template divide the circle in half, as shown at *A*, Fig. 59. Now rule dotted lines downwards and across the base as shown. Take the same radius ($1\frac{1}{2}$ inches) and with *A* as centre describe a quarter-circle. Do the same on the other

side. The resulting shape, coloured black in Fig.
59, is the Scale Template. Cut this out.

To the right is shown how it is used.

Hexagon. To make this describe a circle as

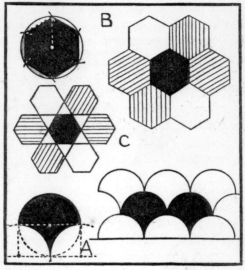

Fig. 59.

before, $1\frac{1}{2}$ inches or as required. The radius of a
circle (in this case $1\frac{1}{2}$ inches) will go six times
round the circumference. Mark off as shown, and
cut out the resulting hexagon. To cut out the
shape in cardboard, use a sharp knife. Also, use a
ruler to keep the cutting straight. Be patient.

Only one model is needed, but it must be true, so if the first is not successful, do another.

At *B*, Fig. 59, is shown how these hexagon shapes are united into what is known as the Honeycomb pattern. A variation of this is shown at *C*, where, in addition to hexagons, there are small diamond shapes. These represent one-sixth of a hexagon, cut like a slice of cake. The template would be made in this way.

Working Models (Fig. 60)

Having cut the template, collect together plenty of thick paper, either brown or white. The template from which the pattern will be built—in this case the hexagon—is then placed upon the paper (see *A*, Fig. 60). The paper is then cut the same shape and size. Quite a number of similar shapes must be cut, each being an accurate reproduction of the original template.

Next cut the pieces of material, using the paper template, but allowing $\frac{1}{4}$-inch turnings all round as at *B*. Be careful to cut to the weave of the material, *i.e.* see that two sides of the hexagon follow either the warp or weft threads of the fabric. At *B* the two sides left and right are straight and follow the warp of the fabric. Failure to do this will produce a patch on the bias, which will look unsightly and puffy when joined.

Lay each patch face downwards, and over it a

G   97

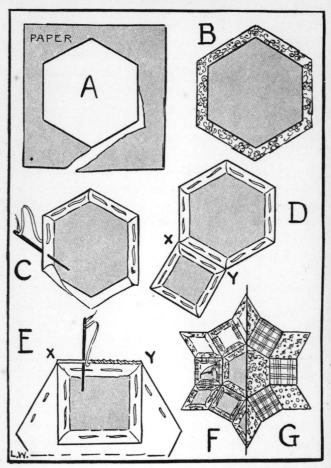

Fig. 60.

paper shape. The material is then turned back over the edges of the paper and tacked, taking the stitches through the paper and material as shown at *C*. Having prepared several patches in this way, they may be joined together in the following manner.

Fit two patches together as at *D*, with the edges *XY* touching. Then overcast these together as shown at *E*, being careful that the needle does not pierce the paper backing. Each patch is joined to the next in this way. When a single patch is entirely surrounded by others, it is sometimes convenient to pull out the tacking threads and remove the papers, as these can be used again. The back of the work with some of the paper backing removed is shown at *F*, and the reverse or front at *G*, Fig. 60.

Notice that at *G* other geometric shapes are shown united into pattern. When the whole article is complete, the final tacking threads and papers are removed and the patchwork is pressed on the wrong side and then lined with suitable fabric. Patchwork is often interlined and then quilted, and in bed-covers this is most effective.

Random Note

In Canadian Patchwork the fabric is folded to ribbon width and arranged in overlapping layers round the four sides of a small square. Several squares are then joined.

English Quilting and Italian Quilting

QUILTING was first inspired by the desire to create warm clothing and bed covering, by means of sandwiching between two pieces of material a layer of lamb's wool. Originally the stitching had no other objective than that of keeping the lamb's wool equally distributed, and prevent it slipping out of position.

The work has still the same objective—warmth. Bed-jackets, dressing-gowns, bed-coverings, etc., are all quilted, and a fashionable use of this work is for cuffs, collars, gauntlets, muffs, etc. The stitchery also has the same objective, but by the 17th and 18th centuries this had become a means of pattern, and with this the principle of *English* Quilting as we know it to-day was firmly established.

ENGLISH QUILTING

Working Materials

All materials that glisten, such as satin, silk or satinette (not the stiff variety), and in light pastel shades, are the best choice, as these lighter shades respond better to the play of light and shade over the undulating surface of the object (see Fig. 61). This is part of the beauty of Quilting and why the work loses much of its charm in dark colours.

The upper material only need be of this expensive class; the under material can be of thin cotton or sateen, but of proportionate weight to the upper material. On quilted garments which are to be

Fig. 61.

lined, this under material can be of fine muslin. The working thread should match the colour of the upper fabric, using strong silk on silken fabrics, and cotton on cotton.

For padding, the modern choice is cotton wadding (first remove the skin). Lamb's wool can still be bought for the purpose. Wool domette, blankets and flannel are also used, and feathers for bed-covers.

Designs

The old Quilting patterns were built up by the aid of the template, one example of this method being given in Fig. 62. This is the Feather Template,

and is shown at the top, in shadow. The quilter draws round the outline of this with her needle upon the fabric and then quilts over the needle-made line. Then another shape is marked and quilted, and so on until the Feather pattern, as shown in Fig. 62, is built. The Scale (see page 96) is another favourite template. Wine-glasses, plates, etc., were also employed. This method of work, especially for articles such as bedspreads, curtains, etc., is to be commended.

Fig. 62.

Transfers can be bought. These should be offset on the back material, and if the material is thin, they can be offset on the wrong side and yet show sufficiently visible for working. If the transfer is offset on the top material, see that the line is very fine, or the stitches will not cover it.

If printed materials are used, the Quilting can be

made round certain portions of the design with good effect. Quilted designs on muslin are also sold. These can be used on cushions and such articles where the back is not exposed.

LESSON

The method of treating the design is the first consideration. If it is to be built by aid of the template, then the " preparation " must be done first. If a transfer (or muslin) is being used, then the

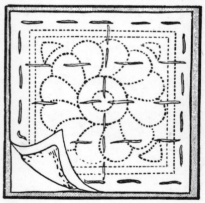

Fig. 63.

transfer must be offset on the back material and the preparation made afterwards. The preparation is made as in Fig. 63.

Lay the satin face downwards on the table, and

over this the padding, and finally the backing material, which carries the design, or vice versa, according to which material, top or bottom, carries the design. Pin all these together once in the centre and then proceed to tack them all together while still flat on the table. Plenty of tacking is the secret of all good quilting (see Fig. 63), as it prevents the different material from shifting. Always start the tacking from the centre, and constantly smooth out the material, tacking horizontally, diagonally and vertically all over the surface.

Stitches

The quilting can be worked either in Back Stitch or Running Stitch, but if a transfer has been offset on the front fabric, then Back Stitch is obligatory, otherwise the transfer line will show. In Fig. 64 is shown Back Stitch which forms an unbroken outline, and in Fig. 65 Running Stitch, which leaves a space between each stitch. Make your choice, but keep to the same stitch throughout.

These stitches when used in Quilting must be formed in two separate movements: (1) down, draw-through thread; (2) up, pull-through thread. This machine-like movement is absolutely necessary, as there are three materials to penetrate. Furthermore, if the design is offset on the back material, this clear and definite method of stitching is the only way of ensuring good results on the front. The length of the stitch is regulated by the thickness of the padding, and these stitches, even though they are creating ornament, must still fulfil their original mission—that of keeping the padding in position.

To commence, make a knot at the end of the thread and bring the needle through to the surface; then pull gently but firmly, and the knot will slip

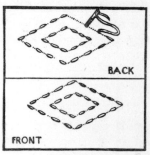

Fig. 64.   Fig. 65.

through the lower layer into the padding, where it will be quite secure. To finish off, make a single Back Stitch and run the needle in through the padding. Cut, and the end will be lost.

When the Quilting is complete, remove all the tacking threads and neaten the edges. The two outer layers of material are turned in and slip-stitched invisibly together. A bed- or cot-cover is often finished with a cord encased in the same material. For articles needing an additional lining, such as a dressing-gown or sachet, both the under layer of material and the padding are trimmed away, and the upper material is turned in to a separate lining and slip-stitched.

ITALIAN QUILTING

In this form of Quilting there is no intermediate filling, as in English Quilting. Two layers of material only are necessary, and the design, which must be in double outline, is covered with stitching taken through both layers, as shown in Fig. 66.

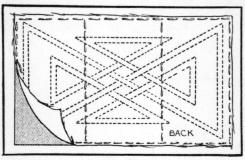

Fig. 66.

This forms a narrow channel, into which a soft cord or thick wool is threaded, thereby throwing the outline of the design into pronounced relief on the front of the article.

The work is used on cushions, cosies, handbags, bed-jackets, cot-covers, cuffs and collars, etc.

On bed- and cot-covers the work is afterwards backed with matching satins, and sewn up the sides like cushions, and a separate pad inserted. This is fastened at the four corners with an occasional stitch or eyelet in the middle, to keep its position.

Working Materials

Silk and satin of the richer kinds, bright or delustred, are most frequently used, but for the under layer butter-muslin will serve. Soft cotton cord or a thick wool for the padding is needed, also a blunt-pointed needle or bodkin with a large eye.

LESSON

Offset the design on to the muslin and lay this over the surface material. The two are then securely tacked together as in Fig. 66, with the traced pattern uppermost. The Quilting is done on the *wrong* side, and in neat, small, running stitches which are made over all the double outlines, as shown in Fig. 66.

The padding also is done from the wrong side. Thread the blunt needle with soft cord or wool of sufficient thickness to well pad the double outline, so that the design will stand out bold and in relief on the front.

Slip the needle between the two layers of material

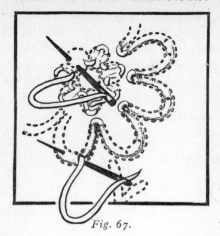

Fig. 67.

Fig. 68.

from the back (see Fig. 67), and thread between the double outline all round the pattern. At any pronounced curve or angle the needle must be brought out and inserted again through the same hole or a little farther along, and the threading continued. Leave the cord loose at any angle to form a small loop (see Fig. 67). This prevents the padding cord from pulling round the corners and spoiling the shape. It also allows for shrinking when washed.

Several Padding Stitches are sometimes needed to fill round shapes, such as is shown at the flower centre in Fig. 68, which also shows the finished effect of the work.

Random Notes

The veil of the Tabernacle is said to have been embroidered in Cross Stitch. Even so, embroidery as a work is still more ancient.

o   o   o

When working on very soft satins or materials difficult to keep straight, first back with vanishing muslin. The stitches are made through this, and when the work is completed use a fairly hot iron, and the muslin will vanish. Iron quickly.

Pattern Building and Honeycombing

SMOCKING is not only a beautiful work, but also the most successful way of controlling width on a garment, as no matter what width the hem of a

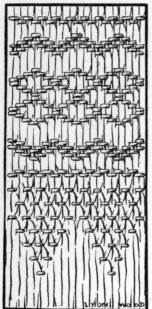

dress may be, if it is smocked at the waist or the yoke it appears graceful and well fitting.

A border such as shown in Fig. 69 could be worked across the front of a child's dress, or in the centre only, or arranged at intervals as small motifs, the latter idea being more prevalent on blouses, dresses, etc., for adults.

Fig. 69.

Working Materials

Almost any fabric, plain or printed, in silk, cotton, linen or wool, can be smocked. The working thread should be of the same texture as the material—that is, linen, mercerised cotton, or silk. Colour is a matter of choice, though it is customary to work with a matching thread, and a beginner is advised to follow this course, as irregularities are not so apparent. Good Smocking looks effective in contrasting colours. On printed materials the dominant colour in the print is a good choice for the working thread.

LESSON

The width of material required for Smocking is approximately three times the width of the finished piece of work. For thicker fabrics rather less, and for fine fabrics a little more, but the multiple of three is a good average. When the material is skimped, the work loses much of its charm. All Smocking should be worked before the garment or article is made up. First, cut out the garment, allowing the necessary extra width for Smocking.

The first process in Smocking is to work several rows of evenly spaced stitches, as shown in Fig. 70, and on the regularity of these depends the success of the work.

With fine fabrics, lay the material on the table, front side down, and on the back mark in a series of evenly spaced dots, using a fine-pointed pencil and ruler. The dots should follow along the grain of the material, for which reason it is necessary to ensure the fabric being straight when cutting out the garment. The spacing of the dots will vary, according to the thickness of the material. On fine fabrics they should be about $\frac{1}{4}$ to $\frac{3}{8}$ inch apart. On heavier fabrics about $\frac{1}{2}$ inch apart. The same distance must be allowed between the rows, as shown at the base of Fig. 70.

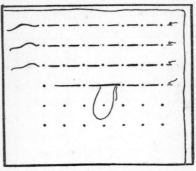

Fig. 70.

A printed transfer, consisting of little dots, evenly spaced in rows, can be bought, and offset on the back of the material if preferred, but care is needed to keep the transfer straight.

On linen fabrics, and on others where the warp and weft are clearly distinguishable, neither dots nor transfers are necessary, as these preliminary stitches can be kept straight by counting the threads, picking up two threads and passing over five—or picking up three and passing over seven, according to the thread of the material. The first space should be measured, and the number of threads then decided upon adhered to throughout.

Foundation Threads

When the dots are completed, these stitches are worked, also on the *back* of the material. Thread the needle with a length of cotton, sufficient to complete one row, as shown in Fig. 70. Make a good-sized knot at the end, as, should the thread slip through later when the material is gathered up, the work will need to be done over again.

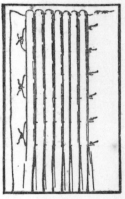

Begin at the right-hand side as shown in Fig. 70, and pick up a small portion of material *beneath* each dot. As each row is completed unthread the needle and leave the end lying loose. When the required number of rows is completed, draw the material up into folds

Fig. 71.

by holding the loose ends of thread in the hand and easing gently along, until the required width for the Smocking is attained. The long ends are then tied firmly together in pairs, close up to the last gathering fold, as shown in Fig. 71, to prevent

H   113

them slipping out of position. The front of the material now presents a series of even "tubes" or "reeds" ready for smocking.

Smocking Patterns

Most smocking patterns are worked from left to right on the right side of the material, using the foundation threads as a guide to keep the smocking stitches straight. The stitch itself is simple, though the methods of grouping and arranging it

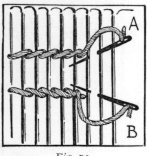

into pattern are almost without end. The most popular methods will be described.

Rope Pattern (Fig. 72).— Commence with a knot at the end of the thread (in Smocking a knot is permissible and necessary) and bring the needle up through the

Fig. 72.

first "tube" on the left. From here pick up a small piece of material on the next tube, as shown at *A*, and repeat on each successive tube, across the width of the work. Keep the thread *above* the needle and insert it in a slanting direction. This produces a rope-like effect twisted to the right. At *B* the same method is shown, but with the needle slanting upwards and the thread *below* the

114

needle to produce a " rope " twisted in the opposite direction.   Rope Pattern can be used in single lines or in groups.

Basket or Cable Pattern (Fig. 73).—The working method is very similar, only the needle is inserted horizontally and the stitches are worked alternately above and below.   Both movements are shown at

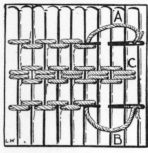

Fig. 73.

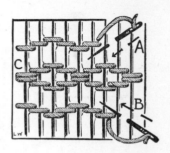

Fig. 74.

A and *B*, while at *C* two rows are stitched close together to give the effect of basket weaving.   The use of this stitch in single lines is shown in Fig. 69.

Chevron Pattern (Fig. 74) is a development of Rope and Basket Pattern, and consists of stitches grouped first upwards and then downwards, and worked with the thread above the needle in ascending, and below, in descending.   Both movements are shown at *A* and *B* with two lines worked in contrary directions at *C*.   Many other such patterns can be achieved by grouping the stitches and lines in different relationship to each other, as in Fig. 69.

HONEYCOMBING

The preparation of this work is similar to Smocking. The fabric is gathered up into tubes as described, and illustrated in Figs. 70 and 71. The working method is shown in Fig. 75. The needle is brought through at the top of a tube, level with a gathering thread. Next pick up a small piece of material from the second and first tubes as seen at *A*. This stitch is drawn quite tightly, after which

Fig. 75.

a second stitch is made just above the first and also drawn firmly. The needle is then inserted at *B* and slipped downwards through the *back* of the tube to the next gathering thread below, and two similar stitches are worked over the second and third tubes, and then back again to the upper line at *C*, this time gathering the third and fourth tubes together. The work continues in this way, first

116

above and then below, using the preliminary lines of gathering threads as a guide throughout.

The Honeycombing can be worked to any width, and can finish with a straight edge, or in points as shown in Fig. 69.

Pressing

When the Smocking or Honeycombing is completed, it should be lightly pressed with a hot iron through a damp cloth, on the back of the work. Next remove the gathering threads and make up the garment.

Random Notes

Florentine work, or Point d'Hongré, is of Hungarian origin, and worked in wool on canvas. The characteristic design is a pointed zigzag line, resembling fork lightning.

o   o   o

There are two favourite ways of treating embroidery design : (1) to embroider the motif and leave the background plain, and (2), to embroider the background and leave the motif plain. This often changes the name of the work, even when the same stitch is used throughout. Cross Stitch becomes Assisi Work, Drawn Fabric Work becomes Rhodes Work, Darning becomes Colbert embroidery.

117

Eyelets, Festoons and Scalloping

This form of embroidery is also known as Eyelet Embroidery, and consists of a series of little eyelets and open spaces, grouped to form a design of festoons and flowers, such as shown in Fig. 76.

Working Materials

The choice of material is rather important because, unless it is of a firm weave, it is difficult to keep the open shapes clear and defined. Experience will overcome this difficulty to some extent, but a beginner should work her first sampler on a firm or dressed linen before experimenting on silk.

The work can be done on muslin, cambric, linen, cotton, silk, crêpe-de-chine or flannel—all of which should be of good quality, as this form of embroidery is hard wearing and will last. On inferior fabrics the work inclines to tear in the wash.

On cotton materials the embroidery should be worked with a cotton, linen or mercerised thread, but no silk, crêpe-de-chine or flannel, with a fine twisted silk. The working thread usually matches the material, but contrasting colours can be used if preferred, though this demands precise and neat stitches as irregularities become more apparent.

Sharp, fine-pointed scissors are necessary, also a stiletto.

Fig. 76.

LESSON

The best way to understand the working methods of Eyelet embroidery is to follow step by step the construction of the design shown in Fig. 76.

Small Eyelets

All eyelets less than $\frac{1}{4}$ inch in diameter are pierced with a stiletto. First run stitch round the traced

Fig. 77.

outline just *outside* the line, as in Fig. 77, then pierce the hole with the stiletto and afterwards cover with fine overcast stitches, as shown.

Large Eyelets

All eyelets larger than ¼ inch in diameter must be cut. First run stitch round the outline as in Fig. 78, and then, using the scissors, snip from the centre vertically and then horizontally. The four points of the material must then be turned under to the back with the needle, and the eyelet overcast, taking the stitches over the folded edge and the running stitches (Fig. 79).

Fig. 78.

The points of the material on the back of the work are afterwards cut away as in Fig. 80.

Oval Eyelets

These form the petals of the flowers in Fig. 76, and are worked in a similar way to the round eyelets, as shown in Fig.

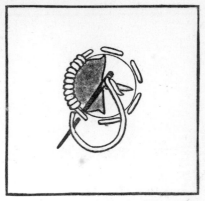

Fig. 79.

81. Care is needed to keep the characteristic shape of the oval—well pointed at one end and rounded at the other.

BACK VIEW

Fig. 80.

Chain of Eyelets

These are shown as curves and festoons in Fig. 76, and are worked a little differently, as their adjacent position renders it necessary for

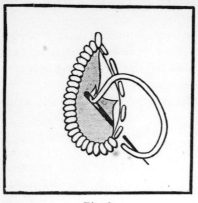

Fig. 81.

extra strength between the eyelets. This is accomplished by making the preliminary running stitches travel first above one eyelet and below the next in a continuous waved journey, as shown in Fig. 82. Here the needle is shown about to begin the return journey, above the eyelet, when it will travel to the base of the

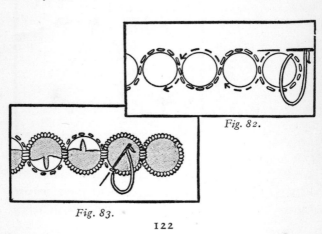

Fig. 82.

Fig. 83.

of the material, and begin a new thread by first making a few running stitches through the padding, and then bring the needle up from below through the loop of the last stitch. In this way an even looped edge is preserved throughout. Finishing-off should be done in the same way.

When the buttonholing is completed, cut away the surplus material close up to the stitches as shown, using very sharp scissors, otherwise the edges will

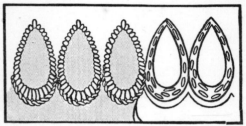

Fig. 88.

present a frayed appearance and quite spoil the work. The four processes—outlining, padding, buttonholing and cutting—are all shown in Fig. 87. This scallop design can be easily evolved by drawing round the outline of a coin.

" Pear " scallop is shown in Fig. 88. This is really constructed of shaded oval eyelets, arranged adjacently in a long row, and worked as previously described, with the exception of the lower edges, which are buttonholed to allow of the surplus material below being cut away.

Simple Cut Work, Renaissance Cut Work and Richelieu Work

THE simplest form of Cut Work is shown in Fig. 89, where all the parts that are in shadow represent open spaces, which are " cut " away after the embroidery is completed. This gives the work a rich appear-

Fig. 89.

ance, and in very elaborate designs the effect is really beautiful.

Designs for such work need careful consideration, in order to ensure that each separate part will tie up securely after the background is cut away. Notice in Fig. 89 how this is accomplished by the overlapping of leaves and flowers, which, while

128

appearing quite natural in effect, are in reality planned to lie thus with deliberation. Were this not so, the design would part when the background was cut away.

Working Materials

It can very readily be appreciated that in a work where half the fabric is cut away, the original material needs to be of a strong, firm quality. Soft materials are not suitable, as they are difficult to cut to a clean edge. For household use—such as sheets, pillow-cases, table mats, cloths, etc.—use a firm linen. If a small-cut work motif is required in silk or crêpe-de-chine, then back the design with organdie and cut it away when the work is completed. This material crisps up the edge for cutting. If vanishing muslin is used, it automatically disappears when it is ironed.

The working thread should match the colour of the linen. This is not obligatory, but it is much more dignified.

LESSON 1

SIMPLE CUT WORK

A glance at Fig. 90 will reveal that the entire design is in double outline, the reason for this being to ensure a correct depth of stitch, which will hold the fabric firm and tidy after the background is removed. All transfer designs for cut work are constructed thus, and all original designs must be based on this principle.

First transfer the design to the linen, and then work two rows of running stitch just inside all the double lines of the design to strengthen the edges, as in Fig. 90, where the needle at letter *A* is shown

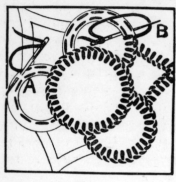

completing the second journey. These stitches must not be pulled tightly at any angle, otherwise the work will pucker. Their object is to keep the covering stitches in position after the background is cut away. When the

Fig. 90.

run stitching is completed, the double line is covered with buttonhole stitch as at *B*, Fig. 90.

Before commencing this, study the design, in order to be certain that the corded edge of the stitch is worked so that it faces that part of the design which is to be later cut away. This is very important, and it is equally important to work the buttonhole stitches close together, otherwise the work loses much of its dignity and appears frayed when cut.

When the buttonhole stitching is completed, the background is cut away as shown in Fig. 91. This is done on the *right* side of the work, using very sharp embroidery scissors, and cutting close up to the buttonholing, otherwise the edges will " fluff "

Fig. 91.

up and spoil the appearance of the work. Careful cutting is essential if the work is to be a success. Compare the three different flower centres, shown in Fig. 91. That at *A* looks very poor compared with the others, and only because it is badly cut.

LESSON 2

RENAISSANCE WORK

Fig. 92 shows another kind of cut work, which is far more elaborate in appearance than that just described, though really not so difficult to work as it looks. A study of this drawing will reveal that the " tie-ups " are no longer made by overlapping portions of the design, but by means of " Bars " or " Brides," which are arranged at strategic points to hold the fabric forming the design in position. Renaissance work is then Cut Work, with the addition of bars.

Fig. 92.

Fig. 92 is rather an elaborate example, and the student is advised to commence with a simpler design in which fewer bars are used, and regard this more elaborate form as an inspiration for later efforts.

The method of working the bars is shown in Figs. 93 and 94. With the exception of this addition of bars, the work remains the same as Simple Cut Work.

The embroidery can start at any convenient point on the design by working the outer row of running stitch as before (Fig. 90), but upon reaching the position for the first bar, the thread must be carried across to the opposite side, as at *A*, in Fig. 93. Here a small piece of material is picked up within the

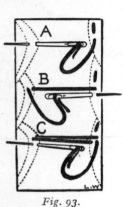

Fig. 93.

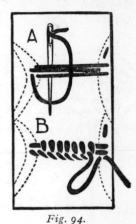

Fig. 94.

double lines of the design to form a tiny stitch. Return as at 93, *B*, and make another stitch, and yet a third stitch as at 93, *C*. The three threads now thrown across the material are closely covered with buttonhole stitching, keeping the bar quite firm, but detached from the material beneath as at *A*, in Fig. 94. Upon reaching the starting point again, continue the running stitch as before until the next bar is thrown.

133

When all the bars are completed in this way, the inner row of running stitching is worked, and finally the design is buttonholed as directed in Simple Cut Work. The final task is cutting away the background, which must be done with care. Cut beneath all the bars, which must be left intact to strengthen the designs, and at the same time add further grace to the embroidery work.

LESSON 3

RICHELIEU WORK

This form of Cut Work is very similar to Renaissance Work, only more rich and lacy in appearance, as the " Bars " or " Brides " are decorated with Picots. This is the only difference. In all other

Fig. 95.

respects the work and the design can be the same as for Renaissance. How to make a bar with a Picot is shown in Fig. 95. This is the most popular method, and known as Loop Picot. The bar is

134

thrown as explained in Figs. 93 and 94. After buttonholing to the centre of this bar, a pin is inserted into the material, as shown in the diagram; and the working thread is first slipped over the head of the pin from left to right, then up over the bar and out beneath it. Fig. 95 should be studied carefully to see just how the needle is slipped under this loop on the pin, and also how the working thread is looped once round the needle-point before it is pulled through. The thread must be pulled tightly to secure the picot, after which the pin can be removed and the buttonholing continued. A finished picot is shown to the right of Fig. 95. Picots such as this can be used at intervals of $\frac{1}{4}$ inch on long bars.

Random Note

The old Peruvians used the feathers of tiny humming-birds to make decorative borders and mantles of state.

DRAWN THREAD WORK

Borders, Corners and Wheels

THIS is a favourite method of finishing both large and small household articles, also scarves, handkerchiefs and linen dresses.

LESSON

A straight border of hemstitching is simply prepared as follows.

Allow sufficient depth of material for the necessary hem, and then withdraw the first thread. To do this slip the point of a pin under the thread which marks the commencement of the border, somewhere near the edge of the material, and ease out an end long enough to be held quite firmly. Withdraw this across the full width of the material, and continue withdrawing other threads in this way, until a border the required depth is obtained. Next turn up the hem close to the edge of the drawn border and tack in position. At this point the work is then ready for the decorative stitching.

This can be worked with the threads of the material just withdrawn, or with fine cotton or silk, varying according to the fabric in use. Never use a heavy-working thread.

Four-sided Borders

These are arranged on all four sides of a square, and present a problem at the corners which makes the drawing process a little more complicated. First plan the depth of the hem as before, and then mark the four spots where

Fig. 96.

the four outer corners of the border will fall. These points represent the limit to which the threads are withdrawn. The first thread to be withdrawn must then be cut 2 to 3 inches away from the marked point, doing the same at both ends, and this short length is then pulled out from the corners (see

Fig. 96). Here it is left for the moment, and the remaining portion across the centre is withdrawn.

Other threads are then withdrawn round all four sides of the square in this same way, until a border

Fig. 97.

the required depth is achieved. The loose-hanging threads as shown in Fig. 96 are then tidied up, in either of the following ways: (1) by cutting them off close to the edge and covering with buttonhole or overcasting stitch, or

(2) by securing the ends between the hem. This is a much better and stronger method (see Fig. 97). The threads are first cut to an even length and tacked. Later, when the hem is turned, they will be completely hidden.

To Mitre a Corner

Each corner must now be finished with a mitre join, otherwise it will be too bulky. The hem is first turned up and the folds are creased with the thumb-nail (see Fig. 98). Now take a pencil and mark spot *B* on Fig. 98, which indicates the corner of the cloth *after* the hem is finished. Fold over the

corner so that it falls along the dotted lines and mark
the crease *A*, *B* and *C* as indicated. Unfold the

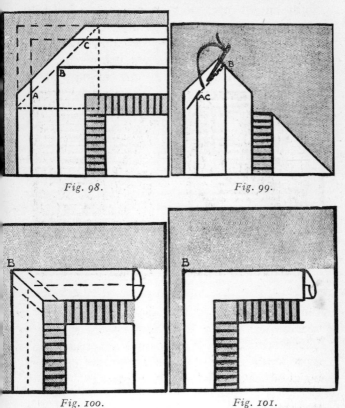

Fig. 98.

Fig. 99.

Fig. 100.

Fig. 101.

material and cut away the corner, just beyond the
creased line, as shown. Fold the cut edges to-

gether, as in Fig. 99, so that *A* and *C* meet, and back stitch firmly down the crease-mark from *B* to *AC*. Finish the stitching at *AC*, as the portion beyond is left for turnings. The seam is now opened out and the corner reversed. Turn under the raw edges, and the hem will automatically fall along the drawn thread border as in Fig. 100, and here it is tacked.

Fig. 102.   Fig. 103.

The dotted lines in the diagram represent the turned edges of the linen now hidden within the folded hem. The professional appearance of a mitre-joined corner is shown in Fig. 101, no stitching at all being visible on the right side.

Hemstitching

The decorate method of securing the hem in position is shown in Figs. 102 and 103. Two move-

ments are necessary, as the loose threads are tied into convenient little bundles in one movement (see Fig. 102), and the hem is secured in the second movement (see Fig. 103). Upon arriving at the open square in each corner, change to buttonhole stitch. This must be worked close together over both edges of the hem, until the loose threads are again reached (Fig. 104), when the hemstitching is continued.

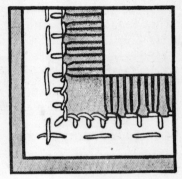

Fig. 104.

A very narrow hem can finish at this stage, but a wider border will need further decoration, so the opposite side of the border must be also hemstitched, taking care that the same bundles of threads are again tied together.

Border Treatment

One of the simplest of the many border treatments is shown in Fig. 105. This is a single twisted border, and worked in the following way, using the same kind of thread as was used for the hemstitching, or just a little thicker, but not much, otherwise it breaks the fabric threads.

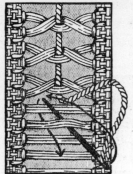

Fig. 105.

First secure the thread in the middle of the buttonholed corner of the cloth, and then take it over the intervening space (see Fig. 106). The needle proceeds over the first two bars (a "bar" being one of the tied bunches of threads), and is slipped back under the second bar, and over the first bar, as shown by the arrows in Fig. 105. The needle is then pulled through and the process repeated all along the border.

Wheels

The wheel shown in Fig. 106 is worked in Back Stitch after all four borders are completed, but the spokes *A* and *B* are formed in the process of working the border. The spoke at *A* is secured into the material and twisted back upon itself to the centre of the wheel, and then carried up to *B* and again twisted to the centre, after which the border is continued as in Fig. 105. To complete the wheel, four extra diagonal spokes must be added and twisted, and then secured in the centre with a

142

single stitch. Back Stitch is then worked, round and round, until the wheel is large enough, then the

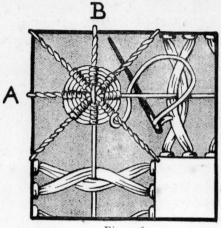

Fig. 106.

thread is slipped in at the back to the centre of the wheel and secured.

LETTERING

For Household, Fashion and Lingerie Use

ALMOST any embroidery stitch can be used to work an initial or monogram, and for household purposes the choice is often Cross Stitch, worked in red linen thread, but an initial will make an excellent ornament, as well as a mark of identification.

A cipher or monogram on a jumper or scarf adds much to its intrinsic value, and on household linen a good letter imparts an air of dignity to bed-linen, table napkins, mats, towels and so forth. A cipher is the name used to describe two letters arranged ornamentally over each other, as in Fig. 108. The letters are both complete. In a monograph the upright stroke of one letter does duty for two letters, so that neither is quite complete.

LESSON

Every woman should have her own initial, monogram or cipher designed for her, and use this as a model for embroidery. It can then be traced off on to any article by placing it in position as required, over carbon paper, and tracing it off. Transfers for single letters can be bought.

Old English Style

Fig. 107 shows an old English letter embroidered in padded Satin Stitch. The working method is as follows :—

The thicker parts of each letter are first outlined with fine running or chain stitches, and then padded between these lines with a bold running or Chain Stitch. Should a highly embossed letter be required, a second layer of Chain Stitch is worked over the first, and possibly a third line or two down the centre. All padding stitches should follow the outline of the letter and continue round and round until the centre is reached. The covering Satin Stitches are then added, and, to prevent

Fig. 107.

puckering, are better worked in an embroidery frame. Make each Satin Stitch slant as shown. Cover the finer lines of the letters with closely worked stem stitching. Ordinary crochet cotton gives a firm solid padding for large letters with the Satin Stitch worked in a good-quality linen thread.

Modern Treatment

Appliqué.

An attractive cipher in Appliqué is shown in Fig. 108. This looks effective on a scarf, jumper or handbag, and should be carried out in a material of contrasting colour. The initials " A. N." are not actually interlaced, although the ingenious way in which the couching thread is laid gives this impres-

Fig. 108.

sion. First draw out the cipher on paper, and then trace on to the material for application. Cut away the background as shown and pin in position and tack (see Appliqué Embroidery). The edges are then overcast with a fine thread and the couching is worked over the edges and carried beneath at any point where the interlaced effect is necessary.

This treatment of Appliqué looks very beautiful on lingerie, using a blue crêpe-de-chine for the letters on pink, or on a chiffon handkerchief, applying the letters in a dark tone of the same shade. If the work is backed with vanishing muslin, it can be done more evenly. This when ironed will vanish away.

Letters without Background

A cipher in Cut Work presents a rich, lacy effect, as shown in Fig. 109. The embroidery is comparatively easy, but the design needs to be carefully planned, as no portion of either letter must hang loose when the background is cut away, otherwise the whole thing will collapse. A clever interlaced effect is shown, using the letters " E. B. S.", " tied up " at each point with a few extra bars for strengthening purposes (see Renaissance Embroidery). First offset on the material, and then outline with Running Stitch, working in any necessary bars at the same time. The letters are

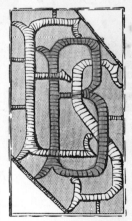

Fig. 109.

then padded as explained in Fig. 107 and covered with Satin Stitches. When all the embroidery is

147

finished, cut away the background. The work is rather fragile, and better used on articles not frequently washed. On delicate fabrics and silk stockingette scarves, first back with organdie and trim away afterwards, or vanishing muslin can be used.

DECORATIVE STITCHING AND FAGGOTING

For Joining, Lengthening and Finishing

DECORATIVE STITCHING is a method of using embroidery stitches so that they perform a practical as well as a decorative purpose. Hems and seams can thus become a medium of decoration, and so add considerably to the appearance of an article or garment, while in no measure failing to perform their practical objective.

The working thread should look important, and repeat in colour any shade used in the embroidery, or else be chosen to match the background. A twisted thread is stronger and preferable.

Decorative Hems

The hem is turned up on the right side of the material, as shown in Fig. 110, and tacked in position, but not hemmed, as it is held quite firmly by the decorative stitching.

At *A* in Fig. 110 the decoration consists of Blanket Stitch, arranged in groups of three, with the looped edge of the stitch to the inner side of the hem.

At *B*, Coral Stitch, of which the working method is clearly shown, is used along the edge of the hem,

and a further decoration of tiny straight stitches arranged in pairs (Dot Stitch), intersected by a single vertical stitch.

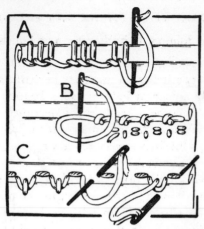

Fig. 110.

At *C*, the hem is first secured with even running stitches of one colour, and these are then linked with a festoon of Fly Stitches worked in another colour.

Uses

A narrow hem of this description is often used to finish the edge of luncheon sets, mats, tea-cloths, etc. Also for narrow hems on sleeve and children's frocks. The suggestion at *B* and *C* could be used on a hem of any depth.

Decorative Overcasting

The working method is as follows, and is completed in two journeys. The two movements of the stitch used for the first journey worked from left to right are shown at *A* and *B* in Fig. 111. At *A*, an upright stitch is overcast into the same spot with the next stitch a short distance to the right, as at

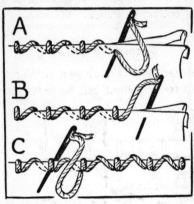

Fig. 111.

B, the thread being carried over and behind the edges of the material, as shown by the dotted lines.

On the return journey, which is worked from right to left, the overcasting is worked as at *C*. The needle is inserted each time at the base of each upright stitch made on the first journey, thus slanting the long stitches in the opposite direction to those made on the first, to form a cross. The

working thread needs to be bold to get the best effect, and the needle fairly thick.

Uses

This is a decorative means of joining the sides of a tea-cosy or cushion, and serves instead of a cord. The stitching would of course be worked round all four sides of the cushion. It can also be used along the edge of collars or cuffs.

Decorative Seaming

Three suggestions are shown in Fig. 112. The two fabrics to be joined can be first run and felled

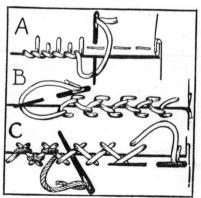

Fig. 112.

together, or evenly tacked together, as shown. After this the material is opened and the decora-

tive stitching worked on the right side of the fabric.

At *A* in Fig. 112 is shown Blanket Stitch, the looped edge being arranged to cover the fold of the fabric. Blanket Stitch is worked from left to right, while Feather Stitch, another suggestion shown at *B*, is worked from right to left.

At *C* is shown Laced Herringbone Stitch. This is worked from left to right. First the Herring bone Stitch is worked as shown by the white thread. After this the herringbone stitches are " laced " with a second thread, of either matching or contrasting colour, as shown.

Uses

Decorative seaming can be used down the seams of garments or for attaching a false hem of matching or contrasting colour. Also for lengthening a garment.

Closed Seams

A narrow hem is first turned on the two fabrics to be joined, as shown in Fig. 113. If a selvedge edge is being united the hem need be folded only once. Two different treatments are shown, (1) with the hems turned on the right side, and (2) with the hems turned on the wrong side.

At *A*, Fig. 113, both hems are turned on to the right side of the material and tacked in position. They

are then joined together with Open Cretan Stitch, worked from left to right, as shown by the needle. Be careful to insert the needle and bring it out again through the double material of the hem, as shown. The stitches must be kept strictly regular and equally spaced apart, as the hem is then further decorated by Blanket Stitches, arranged with the looped edge

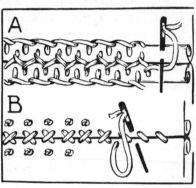

Fig. 113.

along the fold, and the tail of each stitch arranged between each of the Cretan Stitches.

This method of working with the hem on the right side of the material gives a much bolder band effect than that at *B*, where both the hems are turned to the wrong side of the material and then joined with Cross Stitch. A further decoration of French Knots is then arranged over the edge of the hem to keep it in position.

Uses

When a wide band as a decoration is needed to attach material of matching or contrasting colours on runners, curtains, portieres, etc., to join long seams together, such as the side panels on bedspreads. In this case two full widths are used, one of which is split down the middle and joined either side of the central panel. Arrange the selvedge edges to meet, and join as described.

Open Seams or Faggoting

An open seam, such as in Fig. 114, must be prepared in the following manner before any decorative stitches can be added. Turn the raw edges of the material under as for hemming and tack. Keep

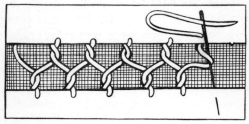

Fig. 114.

the hem narrow and make the first turn as deep as the second. Some workers prefer to slipstitch this in position, though this is not necessary on a narrow hem, as the decorative stitches serve this purpose. Both hems are then tacked to a strip of stout brown paper, leaving a space of about $\frac{1}{4}$ inch or so between, varying this according to the size of the working thread and the material.

The working method is shown in Fig. 114, and is known to dressmakers as Faggoting Stitch, but to the embroidress as Twisted Insertion Stitch. At first glance it appears very similar to Cretan Stitch, but in reality there is considerable difference, as Cretan Stitch is an embroidery stitch and Twisted Insertion Stitch is a lace stitch. Notice how the stitch pierces the material only once, the needle entering from back to front as shown. Each stitch must therefore be held in position by " twisting " the needle under and over the thread before inserting it through the material as shown. In the diagram the stitches are rather widely spaced, to show construction, but they must be close enough to hold the hem straight (or it will wave), and at the same time there must be space enough between each stitch to allow the one on the opposite side to fall between.

Uses

To form seams on delicate fabrics, and patterns with rouleau or ribbon. Principally used on dresses, collars, cuffs and lingerie.

Sprat's Head

The method of working a Sprat's Head is shown in Fig. 115, with the completed Sprat's Head, which forms a triangle at *A*. The outline of the triangle is first chalked on the material round a shape cut out of thin cardboard (the triangle is equilateral, each side measuring about $\frac{1}{2}$ inch). A small

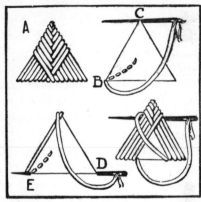

Fig. 115.

running stitch is better worked over the chalked outline for additional clearness, as the chalk line generally disappears. This is afterwards removed.

A fine buttonhole twist, to match the material, is used for working, and the thread, run in from the centre of the triangle, emerges at the bottom left-hand corner (*B*). A small stitch is then made at the apex of the triangle (*C*), and the needle

inserted at *D*, bottom right-hand corner, to
emerge again just inside the first stitch (*E*). The
working continues in this way, taking first a stitch
across the top, just below the last, and then across
the bottom and just within the previous stitch.
In this way each stitch at the top will of necessity
get wider and wider as it descends, while each
stitch at the bottom will become smaller and
smaller as it approaches the middle, until the whole
triangle is filled in and completed as shown at *A*.

Uses

A Sprat's Head is a decorative means of strengthening the top of a box pleat, the broad end being
arranged to face the pleat. Also used to strengthen
the corners of pockets, etc. The motif has a
distinctive tailored look, and is smart on sports
wear, tailored blouses, coats, skirts, etc., and is
often used in its own right, as a decoration.

Transfers

PRINTED transfers are sold in blue, yellow and black print. Yellow is satisfactory only on black material. Blue is the best colour for all light shades. Black is better for blue, green or brown materials.

To Off-set a Transfer

Place the transfer with the shiny side downwards and iron over with a hot iron. An indistinct outline is frequently the result of using the iron too cold. As a test, iron off the trade mark (which must always be carefully removed or disaster results) on an odd scrap of similar fabric, or on the back of the work. If the transfer appears to be sticking, place a damp cloth over it and run a hot iron over the surface again.

In off-setting a printed transfer on rough or coarse material, first press the fabric with a hot iron through a damp cloth. This temporarily flattens the surface. The transfer should be laid over quickly, before this has time to rise again, and the iron held for a second or two in different places until the whole surface has been covered, as the usual ironing movement is not sufficient. If, in spite of these precautions, the outline remains undefined, then it must be strengthened on the fabric with paint, over the faint impression. Use a fine brush and Chinese white.

Frames

The mounting of embroidery into a frame is technically known as " dressing " a frame.

The simplest type is the circular or tambour frame, constructed from two rings of wood which fit over each other, the outer provided with a

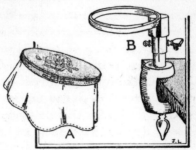

Fig. 116.

tightening screw. Fig. 116 shows the kind with the material already mounted, and at *B* a similar frame fixed into a table clamp. This secures it in position and leaves both hands free to manipulate the work. Circular frames are more suitable for working small designs, and for use in larger patterns, care must be taken in changing the position of the ring, otherwise the stitching is damaged. This may be partly avoided by inserting a piece of soft material between the two rings. Place the inner ring on a table, and over this the material to be embroidered, and over this a piece of protective muslin, and then the outer ring and tighten the screw. Cut away the protective material to within half-an-inch of the rings. This leaves the under material exposed for embroidery, but protected from the rub and pressure of the rings. Should a fine material tend to sag in work, bind the inner ring with a strip of tape, to form a better grip.

Washing and Ironing

Most modern embroidery threads will stand washing and, provided the material is also of a washable nature, the work can be laundered without any qualms. Dissolve pure soap or good soap flakes in hot water and afterwards dilute with cold until little more than lukewarm. Immerse the embroidery and move gently about, but do not rub. Next rinse in warm and then cold water. Dry quickly. Iron on the *wrong* side, placing the work face downwards on to an extra thick blanket so that the embroidery is not flattened out with the iron. (Test to see that it is not too hot.) A damp cloth placed over the work will prevent any possibility of singeing.

To wash delicate embroideries, soak overnight in strong salt and warm water (provided of course the colours are fast). This will remove a great deal of surface dirt, after which carefully immerse in soap and warm water, and move very gently with the hand, but never rub. Roll up in a towel and iron as described.

INDEX

APPLIED Work, 83
Appliqué, 83
   ,,   Felt, 85
   ,,   Net, 91

Bars, 133
   ,,   Picot, 134
Broderie Anglaise, 118

Cipher, 144
Colour, 15
Couching, 52
   ,,   Roumanian, 53
Cross Stitch Embroidery,
   63
Cut Work, 128
   ,, ,, Simple, 129

Darning Embroidery, 77
   ,,   Huckaback, 80
Decorative Hems, 149
   ,,   Overcasting,
     151
   ,,   Seaming, 152
   ,,   Stitching, 149

Eyelet Embroidery, 118
Eyelets, Chain of, 121
   ,,   Edge, 124
   ,,   Large, 120
   ,,   Oval, 121
   ,,   Small, 119

Fabric choice, 12
Faggoting, 155
Frames, 160

Hemstitching, 140
Heraldry, 69
Hexagon, 96
Honeycomb Pattern, 97
Honeycombing, 116

Ironing, 161

Knot, Bullion, 50
   ,,   French, 49

Lettering, 144
Lingerie, 88

Mitre, 138
Monogram, 144

Needles, 10

Patchwork, 93
   ,,   Geometric, 95
Pattern, Basket, 115
   ,,   Cable, 115
   ,,   Chevron, 115
   ,,   Rope, 114
Point Turc, 89
Porto Rico Rose, 52

INDEX

Quilting, 100
,,   English, 100
,,   Italian, 106

Renaissance Work, 131
Richelieu Work, 134
Roumanian   Embroidery,
    75

Scallop, Pear, 127
Scalloping, 126
Seams, Closed, 153
,,   Open, 155
Shading, 124
Smocking, 110
Sprat's Head, 157
Stitch, Back, 25
,,   ,,   Threaded, 26
,,   Blanket, 31
,,   Buttonhole, 32
,,   ,,   Closed,
                34
,,   ,,   Wheel,
                33
,,   Chain, 38
,,   ,,   Detached, 40
,,   ,,   Magic, 41
,,   ,,   Open, 41
,,   ,,   Zigzag, 39
,,   Cretan, 31
,,   Cross, 66–67

Stitch, Daisy, 40
,,   Darning, 79
,,   Feather, 35
,,   ,,   Closed, 36
,,   ,,   Double, 37
,,   ,,   Single, 34
,,   Fly, 42
,,   ,,   Filling, 43
,,   Hem (Sham), 30
,,   Herringbone, 29
,,   Holbein, 24
,,   Lace, 89
,,   Long and Short, 48
,,   Overcast, 44
,,   Pekinese, 26
,,   Running, 22
,,   ,,   Whipped,
                23
,,   Satin, 45
,,   ,,   Padded, 47
,,   ,,   Surface, 46
,,   ,,   Whipped, 47
,,   Stem, 27
,,   ,,   Filling, 28

Templates, 102
,,   Feather, 102
,,   Hexagon, 96
,,   Scale, 95

Washing, 161
Wheel, 143

The E.U.P. Speaker and Debater. Adapted and modernised from "Gibson's Handbook for Literary and Debating Societies," by Rodney Bennett, M.A.

This is a standard work for all those who wish to take part in debate or know how to address meetings. It has been brought thoroughly into line with present-day needs.

The E.U.P. Teach Yourself Latin

'Why Latin?' has been one of the battle cries of the century wherever educationalists meet, but they have managed to adduce some excellent reasons for continuing to learn it. This book covers the groundwork with quite remarkable clarity.

THESE ARE ON THE WAY

The E.U.P. Bell's Standard Elocutionist

This classic work of reference for elocutionists has been brought thoroughly up to date, and will be as helpful to present-day students as it was proved to be to the last generation.

The E.U.P. Teach Yourself German

The same may be said of this book as of *Teach Yourself French*. Enough is here to enable you to go abroad without feeling at a loss and to encourage you to go on reading for pleasure.

The E.U.P. Household Doctor

This is a 'Teach Yourself' book that will be invaluable to everybody outside the medical and nursing professions. As well as the daily minor ills and mishaps, you are bound at some time to be called upon to face real emergencies of illness or accident, and may have bitter cause to regret your lack of knowledge. This book will guide you in the major as well as the minor crisis, and by mastering its wise instructions in hygiene you will avoid preventable illness.

The E.U.P. Teach Yourself To Cook

It is no coincidence that the palm for culture and for cooking is by general consent awarded to the same race. To be a good cook is certainly one of the most useful of all achievements, and Mrs. White has provided a most practical manual in a small compass.

The E.U.P. Teach Yourself Chemistry

With fresh wonders of growth and mechanistic invention being unfolded every day, there is not time for people who are not specialists to acquire more than about a ten-thousandth part of the available knowledge in the many fields of science. But even that knowledge can very materially affect your ability to feel at home in your surroundings, and in the field of chemistry this book supplies just the sort of outline that is wanted.

THESE ARE THE FIRST TITLES

The Student's Guide by Sir John Adams, M.A., LL.D.
Revised and with a Foreword by Rodney Bennett, M.A.

The Student's Guide is inevitably the first book in the series because it is in a sense the key to the others. Many people are diffident about tackling even the most clearly written book of self-instruction, because they really do not know just how to set about it. *The Student's Guide* will clear up all their difficulties. They will find in it a very human understanding of the trials that beset them, and most practical help and encouragement, so that studying alone will become an adventure.

The E.U.P. Teach Yourself French

By the time you have mastered the contents of this book you should know enough French to make yourself understood when you go abroad, and have a groundwork which will enable you to read with sufficient ease to become fluent with continued practice.

The E.U.P. Teach Yourself Mathematics

It is possible to go through life with no more conscious knowledge of mathematics than that two and two make four. Possible, but how much better not to! For an understanding of the simple fundamental laws of mathematics is an extremely valuable part of any mental equipment, and will enable you to think much more clearly on seemingly unrelated matters. This book gives as much mathematical knowledge as is likely to be necessary in any ordinary daily life.

The E.U.P. Teach Yourself Embroidery

Mary Thomas is perhaps the greatest living authority on this subject, and certainly no expert has a greater talent for clear and witty teaching by text and diagram. Embroidery is one of the oldest of the arts, but its place is as secure to-day as ever it was, for machine culture is paradoxically increasing our pride and satisfaction in our own handiwork.

The E.U.P. Teach Yourself Good English

Far too few of us handle our mother tongue really competently. Those dreadful circumlocutions in our business letters; those laborious efforts to make our meaning clear in technical reports ! Yet every reasonably intelligent person should be able to express himself in writing clearly and forcibly—and so he can if he will take a little trouble. This book does not lay down a vast number of those wearisome rules that are proved by their exceptions, but suggests how pitfalls can be avoided and how an easy style can be developed.

ture is the measure of your ability to tackle any situation that life presents, and though you know the names of all the stars and can recite Hamlet backwards, if you are helplessly defeated before a cut finger or the taps on the gas-stove you have very little claim to call yourself a cultured person.

We are bound to specialise to-day, but we need not grow lop-sided. And *Teach Yourself to Cook* will add as much to the cultural development of the woman graduate with first-class honours as will *Teach Yourself Good English* to the clever engineer who is tongue-tied when he is forced to explain himself to the laity.

Knowledge is readily accessible these days—Evening School, Day Continuation School, W.E.A., Technical College, University Extension Lectures. But you will go to these for the subjects you need to specialise in, and meanwhile there is an evening in the week when you don't want to go out to a class; there is the half-hourly train journey night and morning which you have been apt to regard as waste of time; there is, too, the adventure of tackling something entirely by yourself, of being teacher as well as taught.

DULL TEXT BOOKS ARE DEAD

Nothing could give you greater initial encouragement in tackling a new subject than the attractive appearance of the E.U.P. Books. All honour to our fathers who sucked their learning from those dreary-looking volumes which an earlier age seemed to think a necessary accompaniment of ‘ instruction.’ All honour, but, let us say at once, no emulation ! The E.U.P. Books will embellish the most select of bookshelves. Although they cost only two shillings each, they are beautifully bound in blue cloth of a most attractive and modern design. The type is bold and clear, and helpful diagrams and illustrations are not stinted. They are books to use and to treasure.

BOOKS DESIGNED TO HELP YOU

The E.U.P. Books are designed to help you to acquire for yourself, in many fields, the knowledge that will enable you to have an intelligent understanding of the world you live in, and therefore to live a richer life.

We make no foolishly extravagant claims for them. You cannot from a small book learn all there is to know about anything! But you can, from books as clearly written as these, learn enough to be of very practical use and interest to you in your daily life.

EXPERT TEACHERS HAVE MADE THEM

Not all these books are entirely new. Some of them are based on a series of Self Educators published earlier in the century, under the editorship of that great scholar, educationalist and humanist, Sir John Adams. These books were written by expert teachers and they have now been thoroughly revised and modernised by other experts.

Clarity and simplicity is their keynote, both in style and in the development of the subject. The student cannot and will not wish to avoid effort in learning, but these books have been carefully designed to spare him *fruitless* effort.

BALANCE YOUR KNOWLEDGE

In looking through the list that follows, it will be seen that not all the books are on ' academic ' subjects. This is an essential part of the plan of the series. These books are designed for everybody, and they are designed for use in living, not to enable you to decorate yourself with a little snobbish ' learning.' The test of your cul-